D0112160

Loving What Doesn't Last

AN ADORATION OF THE BODY

Loving What Doesn't Last

AN ADORATION OF THE BODY

Christina Kukuk

Morehouse Publishing
NEW YORK

Copyright © 2021 by Christina Kukuk

All rights reserved. No part of this book may be reproduced, stored in a retrieval system, or transmitted in any form or by any means, electronic or mechanical, including photocopying, recording, or otherwise, without the written permission of the publisher.

Unless otherwise noted, the Scripture quotations contained herein are from the New Revised Standard Version Bible, copyright © 1989 by the Division of Christian Education of the National Council of Churches of Christ in the U.S.A. Used by permission. All rights reserved.

Scripture quotations marked "CEB" from the COMMON ENGLISH BIBLE. © Copyright 2011 COMMON ENGLISH BIBLE. All rights reserved. Used by permission. (www.CommonEnglishBible.com)

Morehouse Publishing, 19 East 34th Street, New York, NY 10016
Morehouse Publishing is an imprint of Church Publishing Incorporated.

Cover design by Paul Soupiset
Typeset by Rose Design

Library of Congress Cataloging-in-Publication Data

Names: Kukuk, Christina, author.
Title: Loving what doesn't last : an adoration of the body / Christina Kukuk.
Description: New York, NY: Morehouse Publishing, [2021]
Identifiers: LCCN 2021023772 (print) | LCCN 2021023773 (ebook) | ISBN 9781640654112 (paperback) | ISBN 9781640654129 (epub)
Subjects: LCSH: Human body--Religious aspects--Christianity. | Theological anthropology--Christianity. | Incarnation.
Classification: LCC BT741.3 .K85 2021 (print) | LCC BT741.3 (ebook) | DDC 233/.5--dc23

LC record available at https://lccn.loc.gov/2021023772
LC ebook record available at https://lccn.loc.gov/2021023773

For my mother, my first teacher
For my Beloved
For our children most of all

Contents

I. BIRTH

II. FOOD

III. PLEASURE

IV. PAIN

V. DEATH

VI. WATER

Acknowledgments

This book began with a poem and the desperate hope that one particular body might not be forgotten. Deepest gratitude to Carla Durand and *Bearings Online* for first publishing "Organ Donor" in July 2016 and to Graham Fender-Allison for being its first audience years before in Glasgow.

Bringing a book to life takes a whole lot of people, of course, and this one owes its existence to the rich and unpredictable communities created by the Glen Workshop and the Collegeville Institute. I especially want to thank Natasha Oladokun, Harrison Scott Key, Mary Potter, and Debbie Blue for creating spaces of affirmation and courage. Everyone who sat with me around the tables they prepared brought some gift that made this book and my writing better.

I would have given up on sharing this work long ago if not for the steady encouragement of my writing partner Rosalind Hughes. Our work sessions are a lifeline. And every first-time author should be lucky enough to have an editor who believes in their work the way Milton Brasher-Cunningham believed in this project. Thank you to him and the entire team at Morehouse Publishing for caring so deeply, not only about the words but also about those who write them.

Special thanks go to my friend Michael Glass, the doctors and nurses in my family, and to several small-town funeral home directors, all of whom humored my odd and randomly timed questions about human anatomy and medical practice. Many thanks also to Julie DeMareo and the chaplains of Loyola University of Chicago's Health Sciences Campus Ministry as well as Bruce W. Newton, chair of anatomy at Campbell University's School of Osteopathic Medicine.

I am forever honored by the members of congregations in Minnesota, Ohio, and Oregon who trusted me and welcomed me into some of the most vulnerable moments of their lives. Although most names and many identifying details were changed to honor that trust and protect personal privacy, this is a work of nonfiction.

I'm grateful for the friendship of Donna and Melissa, who sustained me with gifts of green tea and origami. My spouse and children keep me from going hungry or taking myself too seriously. Thanks go in particular to my now-thirteen-year-old who found a draft of these acknowledgements in the printer tray and helpfully edited it so it did not sound "so dead."

Prologue

Sometimes I blame being raised by a surgical nurse for my adoration of the body. Each time a new edition of the *AORN Journal* ("The Official Voice of Perioperative Nursing") arrived at our house, my teenage self studied the before and the after. Before, sometimes the skin bore marks of surgical ink. "Cut along the dotted line." After, the tissue might pucker with stitches or staples, but it clearly claimed its way back to being made whole. I could flip through those journals for hours, fascinated by the human body: its wounds, its diseases, its ability to stretch, to open, and to mend.

Developing human embryos all have the same genitals until the sixth week of gestation, when genetics and hormones begin organizing all the parts into differing configurations we classify as male and female, sometimes imperfectly.

The human liver is the only organ that can regenerate. Because it can grow more of itself, we can lose a lot of it and still survive.

When our bodies finally shut down, the cells of the retina, I have learned, are some of the first to die. We lose the ability to hear last, which is why we keep talking to the unconscious and the comatose.

Why in the name of anything approaching holy does this matter? Do our bodies matter?

For a couple millennia, some of the loudest and most powerful voices said no—or, at the very least, they insisted that these bodies are shells we work to leave behind, like an earthly chrysalis broken open by a butterfly soul flying off to heaven or dead skin rubbed off after a sunburn to reveal tender pink and brand new epidermis beneath. The body was seen as a means to a spiritual end instead of the very habitation of the holy. My own religious tradition, entangled with Western colonialism and white superiority, remains exceptionally guilty of such a view. The apostle Paul did not start the denigration, but he illustrated it as well as any. As an earnest preacher grasping

1

for metaphors in a world built on dualism, he saw the body as sin and death, and the spirit as life and righteousness.

"Wretched man that I am!" Paul wrote, "Who will rescue me from this body of death?"

Some days, I can relate.

Human bodies have gotten no easier to live in since Paul first wrote. For all their assistance, advances in medical technology have made managing our bodies more fraught and complicated with each generation.

Paul and I share the same line of work and some of the same theology, but in a world where every woman is grappling with the gendered violence carried in her muscle memory, where our school-age children are taught to recognize their amygdala response on the playground, where everyone who works with people is retraining themselves to recognize adverse childhood experiences and the lasting trauma they write into growing brains, some part of our message that "the Word became flesh and lived among us" begs for reclamation.

One day, I rested my hands on the top of my thighs and felt in that simple act of self-compassion two severed halves of me were being made whole. With my body and not with my intellect, I comprehended in that moment that all the theology that had fed the dualism and division between body and spirit, though dressed in religion, was anything but holy.

We are only matter, in the cosmic sense. Bodies birth other human bodies to life through blood. We eat and bathe, embrace and ache, expire—eventually—and the dust of our bones washes away into the water table.

But as our particular story goes, into the dust of the ground the Holy One blows the breath of life. And the human comes to life. In a body.

I: BIRTH

1. BIRTH

Bearing from Before to After

The last time I saw Jane's face, her forehead and cheekbones bore bruises from the bloody eruption in her brain, sores flared in her nose where the feeding tube had been threaded through, and her lips peeled away in cracked, papery flakes. Those wounds did not unnerve me. Her eyes did. When she saw me, recognition flashed through them, then memory (I supposed) of what my presence meant or could mean.

I tried to smile, to reassure, to pray, and to bless. But I couldn't take away the fear.

And who could blame her? I had buried her husband not six weeks before, closing long years of days darkened by a tumor. She had stood near me, weeping, as I blessed and anointed his body, wasted but still animated by circulating blood.

Now she was the one in the hospital bed.

We had been told she was on the mend, so I joked, "These are prayers of thanks and healing, not last rites." She tried to laugh as I smeared the suspicious oil above her brow.

But the face my thumb touched is gone now. Gone within days, leaving behind a stupidly insufficient string of adjectives: extinguished, passed on, snuffed, stolen.

Our bodies green and bloat so quickly. We are fruit with a limited shelf life. Her face so quickly taking on the shade of a bruised Bartlett pear, her eyes closed to light. Perishable. That a religion would claim God chose to get all wrapped up in this thin skin still shocks and surprises. "He was God, and then became man," wrote Athanasius of Alexandria, "and that to deify us."[1] To claim this should make all the difference in how we live and die in these bodies.

---

1. Athanasius, "Four Discourses against the Arians," Discourse I, Ch. XI, Par. 39, trans. Archibald Robertson, NPNF2-04 (Grand Rapids, MI: Christian Classics Ethereal Library), 329, retrieved June 1, 2021, from Christian Classics Ethereal Library.

I have a groupie's affection for funeral directors. I admit it. After countless hours in a hearse, killing time picking the brains of morticians, my admiration for the care and compassion the good ones give only grows. I marvel at their work with corpses. The technical skill. The surgeon's precision. I file away the equally heroic and uncomfortable facts of organ donation. For example, tissue recovery technicians always replace organic material with some synthetic approximation. But the human circulatory system is a closed circuit, difficult to seal once opened. In a town where embalmed, open-casket viewings are the norm, the devil could live in these details—and really spook a family without the tactful intervention of a good funeral home.

In five and a half years of pastoring in one church, I performed a funeral almost every month. Each forehead, each hand, began to feel unbearably precious. I wondered if I could trace the origin of that reverence to my surreptitious study of surgical magazines as a thirteen-year-old. Poring over them, I grasped with a kind of ignorance some sense of the words I've since prayed from a fraying book most Wednesdays for a decade:

> O God of heaven, you have made your home on earth
> in the broken body of Creation.
> Kindle within me
> a love for you in all things.[2]

A dead body differs so much from a living one. Even an almost-dead, rasping carcass, the kind whose flesh seems to jump the gun on its disintegrating job days, weeks, or months before the heart stops. Even these bodies live, often stubbornly so.

Miriam's yellow wax-bean face, propped up with a towel by the hospice nurse until her two daughters could get there, and her father's face, propped in almost the same pose a few weeks later in a room just across the hall, both differed from the not-yet-dead. They were alive. And then, in what felt like moments, they were not.

---

2. J. Philip Newell, *Celtic Prayers from Iona* (Mahwah, NJ: Paulist Press, 1997), 44.

A person can bear to care for the body on one side of the Great Divide or the other, and even rejoice in the work, but I may never grow used to shouldering a body as it crosses from before to after. No dotted line of surgical marker directs the way to fixing this.

"For we too are [children] and gods by grace," another powerful church man of Alexandria once wrote, "and we have surely been brought to this wonderful and supernatural dignity since we have the Only Begotten Word of God dwelling within us."[3] I weigh the arm or hand or head I chance to cradle in my own perishable palm, and I can only pray.

---

3. Cyril of Alexandria, "On the Unity of Christ," trans. John McGuckin (Crestwood, NY: St. Vladimir's Seminary Press, 1995), 80.

Body Count: Mary Had a Baby

t's just baby toes. One December, I find myself gazing at a blurry black and white photograph of an infant's feet and guessing that I'm supposed to feel warm and fuzzy. At the sight of those little piggies, I am expected to slip into baby talk, gushing over chubby toesie woesies. It is December, when dimpled babies kill Christmas with cuteness. I'm supposed to caption this photo for a writing assignment.

I check myself: What do I really feel?

Progressive Christian folks avoid focusing too much on the baby at Christmas. It's not just kind consideration for the bereaved parents or those who are unwillingly childless. You could make a solid case that Christmas is more about the end of the world—as we know it—than it is about the little squirt who soiled those swaddling clothes. The sparse infancy stories in our Bibles make a pretty pathetic baby album for Jesus.

Then there are mothers like me who look at that photo of baby feet and think not, "How shall we receive the Christ child this year?" but rather, "Have they digitally altered that kid's toenails, or are my infants the only ones who came out with gnarly talons?" Caring for actual infants 24-7 stretches nativity sentimentality beyond credibility. Whoever wrote that "little Lord Jesus, no crying he makes" was not a parent. Babies are loud. And they stink. One may nuzzle your neck sweetly and a second later regurgitate their sour milk vomit into the open neckline of your shirt, down into your bra, and right between your breasts. For these reasons and others, I don't focus much on the baby either.

Except one year, when singing "Mary Had a Baby" felt like proclaiming a revolution.

It was 2013, the year three transgender women were murdered in Cleveland.

The day the first story broke, I cried and couldn't focus on work. The early edition of the newspaper for the western suburbs included a description crude enough to make any mother howl. Cemia "CeCe" Dove, twenty years old, had been stabbed forty times; her body was discovered in a retention pond where it had been submerged, tied to a concrete block. Something was wrong with the way the body was described, more as an object than someone's child. A violence committed again in print. She was twice dehumanized. It was not only her body that got mangled. Initially, the police and the newspaper mangled her story, too.[1]

I sat at my dining table and started to sob. Why did it hit me so viscerally? Was it only that I felt the vulnerability of my children, one toddling and one bright-eyed and loving every minute of preschool? Or was it because one of my first and dearest colleagues in ministry was a wise, thoughtful trans man with a deep faith in Jesus? Later that year, a month after a jury sentenced CeCe's murderer to life in prison, people gathered to grieve and speak out for two more murdered trans women, Brittany and Betty.

My body is a white body, my skin a peachy-pink. My flesh is more protected than CeCe's, even from birth, and is almost never compared to food or drink in print. People describe my people's skin as white, like snow or wool. Elemental, not edible. Even after an enviable trip to the Caribbean or the Keys, we are "bronzed," not caramel or coffee or chocolate. And Baby Jesus? Well, for centuries, colonizing Christianity, the faith that shaped my childhood, depicted the infant holy only as a golden-haired and blue-eyed white child.

---

1. Michael Sangiacomo, "Concrete Block on Body Found in Olmsted Pond," *Cleveland Plain Dealer*, April 20, 2013, *https://www.cleveland.com/metro/2013/04/body_found_in_ olmsted_pond_sta.html*. Print edition received in the western suburbs differed slightly from later edition published online. Again in John Caniglia, "Oddly Dressed Body Found in Olmsted Township Pond Identified," *Cleveland Plain Dealer*, April 29, 2013, *https://www.cleveland.com/ metro/2013/04/body_of_oddly_dressed_man_foun.html*. See also Rachel Dissell, "Andrey Bridges Sentenced to Life in Prison in Stabbing Death of Transgender Woman," *Cleveland Plain Dealer*, November 13, 2013, *https://www.cleveland.com/court-justice/2013/11/andrey_bridges_ sentenced_to_li.html*, and Regina Garcia Cano, "Cleveland Police: Recent Slayings of Transgender Women Are 'Crimes of Hate,'" *Cleveland Plain Dealer*, December 15, 2013, *www.cleveland. com/metro/2013/12/cleveland_police_recent_slayin.html*.

It's popular in my new neck of the woods to divide the divine from the human in Jesus, to embrace the guy but not the God. I get it. I really do. Half of Jesus's real-life followers wouldn't have called him "God." Despite centuries of clerics decrying such Docetism as heresy, I can't blame a rational human for finding the "fully God and fully human" claim hard to swallow. If, for the ancients, the offense was God becoming human, our contemporary intelligence gets insulted by a human becoming God. Or at least only one man becoming God.

Yet I wonder how much more reverently we would treat the skin, hands, feet, faces, limbs, and wombs of Brown bodies if we really believed God inhabited one for a lifetime. The usual way we glorify the ending of that life—in brutal torture—misplaces the glory for me. It is tragedy, not triumph, writing large across history the inability of individuals and empires to honor the divine in the body of a little Brown boy resisting occupation. The glory is that God is in that body going where we fear so we don't have to be afraid.

A short time after the murders of these three trans women, twelve-year-old Tamir Rice was killed by police in the same part of Ohio. Because the playground where police killed Tamir sat just a few blocks from my friends' house, and because Tamir looked like he could have been our neighbor or my kids' schoolmate, I marched in protest for the first time: to police precincts during the day, hanging on the periphery of the federal building steps for a rally; at night through downtown singing "Carols for Justice," adapting lyrics to sing "O Little Town of Ferguson" and "Away in Ohio" and the Jewish song "Rock of Ages."

It was not the first public outcry over Cleveland police abuse of a Black body. In 2012, thirteen police officers fired 137 bullets at Malissa Williams and Timothy Russell through the windshield of their car in a middle school parking lot. Though police claimed they chased the car at high speeds because they thought they heard a gunshot, there was no gun in the car. Williams and Russell had been residents at homeless shelters in the city. Police tried to pull over their car because it was spotted in a place known for drug deals, despite no traffic violations and nothing coming up on the license plate scanner. Because the driver fled instead, their lives ended in a shower of bullets. One hundred and thirty-seven bullets. Six officers were eventually fired for dereliction of duty, for chasing a car at high speeds despite any threat of violence from its occupants. The city eventually settled with the families for $3 million.

But in 2014 it was a child named Tamir.

In Cleveland, the senses have many places to escape trauma. At least for a little while. A truly great lake, rivers, and nature preserves, along with world-class museums built by steel and rubber barons a century earlier, are frequent day-off escapes. The Museum of Natural History, chock full of children, was where I tried to recalibrate after too late a night following activist friends on social media. But everywhere I moved, I felt the whiteness of my skin, my white mother-ness, the relative skin safety of my white son, whom I sent into one bathroom while I spun into the other to discover only my white self and one Black mother. I battled the urge to say something, anything. What would I say? "I'm sorry." "Can I help?"

I did not say anything. I do think I offered an empathetic smile. In the cavity of my chest, my heart ached, and I felt the individual cells of the skin on my forearms, hands, and face as if whiteness had singed each one. I wondered if the other woman trying to wash her hands, unbothered by my earnest aura, felt anything similar yet different.

The author Thandeka calls the ache of my cells trauma—the trauma left behind by "learning to be white." In her book by that title she proposes that there is a moment in the childhood of every Euro-American when they are "inducted" into whiteness, an initiation instigated and maintained by shame.[2] Assigned to me in a seminary course, I peppered the pages of that book with blue pen marks of both incredulity and conviction. My questions and exclamations deepened in the years that followed with each new hashtag and its aftermath. As I wrestled to understand how the holy might make a

---

2. Thandeka, *Learning to Be White: Money, Race, and God in America* (New York: Continuum, 2000).

home in this body of mine, I had to wrestle, too, with the ways this white body related to Black and Brown bodies, our transcontinental muscle memories, and all the places past and present these bodies intersected in dances of power and violence. I will never ever fully understand what it was like for that Black mother to walk through the Museum of Natural History that day carrying the particular generational trauma of anti-Blackness.

Those were the years I started to sing Odetta's "Mary had a baby . . ." with desperate gusto. I sang not to debate the scientific improbability or the creedal value of a virgin birth. I know why that bit makes a good story. And I don't need other people to believe in the Incarnation—the technical term for God becoming human. I don't even need the members of my faith community to believe it. But I will tell you it's what keeps me following Jesus: There was a man with a body in whom other people met God. The wholly divine became a child of ordinary human beings so that ordinary human beings might become children of God. God took on flesh first in the womb of a woman. Mary had a baby so that here, in my body, I can be holy now—not just after I'm rid of it.

Emmanuel's coming made CeCe's and Betty's and Brittany's and Tamir's flesh sacred long before it was bruised and cut and pierced. I sang "Mary Had a Baby" to insist that and to pray that many more of us would live as the children of God we were born to be—and count every body as holy.

Perhaps that holiness is easier to believe when gazing at an infant. Vincent van Gogh painted the baby Marcelle Roulin three times by herself and twice on her mother's lap in 1888, explaining, "A newborn baby has the infinite in its eyes."[3]

Every body counts: the baby bodies with kissable toes and stinky heads. The elderly bodies we must wipe clean. The saggy bodies with rolls and dimples. The bony bodies with sharp angles and thin skin. The bodies subconsciously coded "dangerous" for no other reason

---

3. *Van Gogh Repetitions* (Cleveland: Cleveland Museum of Art, 2014), published by Yale University Press in association with the Cleveland Museum of Art and The Phillips Collection in conjunction with an exhibition of the same title, organized by and presented at the Cleveland Museum of Art, March 2, 2014–June 1, 2014.

than their pigmentation. The bodies that emerge from a womb to be assigned gender and identity vastly different than their owners know themselves to be. The bodies that discover in middle age childhood wounds that left scars more than skin deep.

Mary had a baby. And every body counts.

Midwife

My first teacher was a midwife. Officially, of course, my mother worked as a registered nurse. She trained and worked in an obstetric unit before finding a better paying job in surgery. Usually, this certified bathing and bandaging and stitching of bodies happened away in a hospital operating room, where I was not allowed to follow her for years. When forced by single parenthood to bring us along on weekend calls where other nurses begrudgingly tolerated us in their locker room, we kids entertained ourselves blowing latex gloves into balloons or donning disposable blue paper slippers while my mother helped some bloody new monkey slip into this world through an emergency hole cut in his mother's womb.

But I knew my mother first as a midwife. And the midwife calls were different. Back in the days of 1980s Jesus hippiedom, my mother gave prenatal care to Amish and Mennonite women in the two counties that surrounded our home on a hill. We'd play in some farm's chicken yard or be left to dream on a wraparound porch or pick berries with the siblings of the unborn. It was just as common, though, to be called to fetch some useful thing or have to knock on the door of the bedroom serving as an exam room with my own urgent childhood need. There, as natural as can be, I would see my mother's hands palpate a fetal skull, rump, or back and measure the fundal height above a tuft of pudendal hair.

These were women's bodies. They nursed and gave birth to live young. I never saw a nursing shawl until I nursed my own children. Then, the suburban mothers who may have flashed their tatas in a bar on Mardi Gras befuddled me by puritanically draping their breasts in blankets while a hungry infant wailed.

I explored my mother's midwifery books with the same curiosity and awe as I did the surgical journals, but they differed. One pictured four nude pregnant women seated in a circle, legs crossed, and garlands on their heads. I studied the long blonde hair tumbling down and past shoulders, the shadows of areolas and pubic hair, the way I later learned to gaze at a Picasso in the art museum. In our sexually repressive religious household, these "private parts" on full display titillated like hidden Halloween candy, the sugar and the supposedly satanic holiday both forbidden to us. But I saw another difference, even if it didn't crystallize in my mind until much later: these women were whole.

The midwifery photographs captured their entirety, from head to toe, even if they squatted or crouched supported by a spouse's arms or lay back beneath a midwife's practiced hands. Unlike the surgical magazines, filled with pieces and parts, one limb, one organ at a time, these women were whole.

In my experience, birth is not magical, but it is full of wonder. Real. And real messy. Thanks to the unpredictable geography of employment, my mother helped me birth both my children. The first time around, I'd been polite, despite the back labor and painful attempts to turn my "sunny-side up" egg from without. Nearly fourteen hours in and finally to the pushing part, the certified nurse midwife charged with my well-being chided, "You're not giving me 100 percent. You need to give me a 100 percent."

Grunting and bearing down yet again, I shot back, "I really feel like cussing at you."

At my attempted retort, she cracked up. A moment of levity.

"She was egging me on on purpose, wasn't she?" I asked my mother later.

"Yes," she confirmed. "She knew it would get a rise out of you, to accuse you of giving less than 100 percent. And she was worried, we both were, that you were wearing out."

I had not quite worn out before pushing that first baby out what medical professionals call "posterior," and the Germans imaginatively describe as "gazing at the stars," and which I experienced as "linebacker baby leading with her shoulder blades, makes bone-cracking tackle past mother's sacrum, coccyx, and pelvic bones."

After that breaking and tearing, I held less back.

When I delivered my son two years later—again during an understaffed holiday shift at the hospital—the official midwife was delayed, but the kid and I were waiting for no one. A nine-pound second baby, he came fast and hard. I held back neither expletives nor emotion, dropping f-bombs audibly and swearing under my breath at the nurses who wouldn't fill the birthing tub without the midwife and who kept chattering like squirrels while they made inane measurements, oblivious that I was already in transition. One still point before the final push stands out. Mom sat outside the birthing tub, holding a cloth soaked with herb-infused ice water to my straining forehead, while I rested my chin against the rim. A foot from my head, she heard from my momentarily closed-eyed silence, a soft, "Ouch. That hurts."

She laughed and asked gently, "What hurts?"

What hurts? My body, stretching and tearing to push the melon-sized head of a nine-pound, four-ounce boy into this world. His big sister certainly made room when she'd obstinately refused two years before to turn under the midwife's hands. Those broken, stretched, and torn places were stretching and tearing once again.

Ouch.

I delivered my children in a wash of so much blood, the staff monitored me for anemia both times and sent my spouse home with specific instructions about steak, broccoli, blueberries, and other iron-rich foods.

You may understand, then, how a translation of Mary's Magnificat disturbed me one December. From the chancel of a stone church, golden members of a baroque orchestra sang in Latin of the glory of the Blessed Mother's membranes. At least, that's what the translation in the program notes indicated: "The Virgin remains intact."

I leaned over to my spouse to point out my disgust with a fingertip and an incredulous eye roll. During intermission, my irritation took on volume.

"Is he talking about the hymen here?" I asked, getting louder. "Is this for real?"

"Apparently," Adam said. "I'm going to get a drink of water. Need anything?"

I muttered an expletive under my breath, newly offended that the Virgin Birth and Matthew's reassurance of Mary and Joseph's celibate union allowed religious men to daintily avoid the blood and mess of birth, of procreation, even.

John Chrysostom, so much my kindred at Easter, sounds strange on Christmas Day, distant and downright odd. "The Father begot in the Spirit and the Virgin brought forth without defilement . . . so neither did the Virgin endure corruption in her childbearing."[1] As if the long stream of the rest of us with wombs defiled and dirtied ourselves to deliver our children to life. Blood, shit, and water: birth is messy. But dirty or corrupt?

In a photograph from the pages of one of my mother's midwifery books, a mother looks toward the reader from a bed backlit by a great picture window, its sill lined with potted plants. We see her from the side, slightly angled, lying against a pile of pillows propped at the headboard. Her knees are parted, newborn baby blanketed against her naked chest. The camera's angle puts one bent knee, calf, and thigh in the foreground, obscuring her genitals, but a narrow trickle of blood lines the inside of the opposite thigh, stopping just above the knee. A splatter on the far calf, another small, bloody constellation behind the far hamstring. Her right heel could be in shadow. Or she could have just finished grinding it in some lost life blood.

The woman's face is turned toward the camera, jaw set, if tired, not smiling, not shying, unbothered by the humid halo of hair loosened by labor from its tie.

"The experience of birthing calls on a woman to shed her social skin and discover a definite feminine power in flowing, accepting and surrendering to natural forces,"[2] the authors note.

She is not defiled.

When it comes to Mary, the Mother of God, Chrysostom sounds ridiculous. How could a mother read this? "And he was born from a virgin, who knew not his purpose . . . neither had she labored with

---

1. John Chrysostom, "The Mystery," *Watch for the Light: Readings for Advent and Christmas* (Farmington, PA: The Plough Publishing House, 2001), 229. An excerpt from "The Joys of Christmas," from *The Living Testament: The Essential Writings of Christianity Since the Bible* (New York: Harper and Row, 1985).

2. Elizabeth Davis, *A Guide to Midwifery: Heart & Hands* (Santa Fe, NM: John Muir Publications, 1981), 2.

him to bring it to pass, nor contributed to that which he had done, but was the simple instrument of his power."[3]

Like hell. She labored. Mary labored, or that Christ child was no human child, but an alien instead. Chrysostom would have us believe that "nature rested while the will of God labored,"[4] that the mother was merely wood a carpenter found and hollowed out to hold a tiny sailor, or the mud of a bank squeezed and shaped into a cup, fired, and dried to fill with wine. Simply a vessel.

A really clean vessel. Immaculate.

Chrysostom is right about the Incarnation in one way only: "Ignomy shall become honor."[5]

I wear the blood and ignomy of birthing with pride. Mary can, too.

---

3. Chrysostom, "The Mystery," 231.

4. Chrysostom, "The Mystery," 230.

5. Chrysostom, "The Mystery," 232.

Pieta

What struck me most about the body was his size. We think of the dead as small, powerless, nearer to invisible than we, but this body hulked across the gurney in the emergency room. Still as stone, it seemed like it might lurch over the bed's edge at any moment, rising with a roar of strength and will. Large chest. Broad shoulders. Light brown hair worn shaggy but not exactly long. The hint of freckles like his mother's. Head lolled to one side, torso twisted away, arms sweeping to the left as if about to roll onto one shoulder and rise.

Of course, it wasn't just a body lying there. It was Matthew. And as if to guarantee against anonymity, a knotted hemp and bead necklace circled his neck, looking already a little too small as the cells and tissues puffed with the water and wastes and gases his organs no longer could expel.

I avoided looking at first. Entering the room on my pastoral comfort mission, I searched first for the living. I set my face toward the mother who was sitting and gazing upon her son. Sturdy farm-wife stock though she was, she couldn't have held him. He was too big. Only after our embrace and a second hug from the daughter who emerged from just behind the door did all of our eyes finally rest on the body in the room.

The good healers left a tray piled high with snacks, their chief resources for patients admitted to the hospital already beyond hope. What help can be given death? Into death's maw hospitals can only shove Fig Newtons and Lorna Doones and tiny bottled waters. I'm not entirely sure my offerings held any greater powers: an oiled fingertip, a prayer, and a song, while we waited outside of time for this holy mother's third child to arrive.

Sometime after that day, I stood before Michelangelo's *Pieta*—the only work he ever signed—and started with recognition at the posture of that holy mother bent over the body of her sprawling adult child. Marks of torture do not loom large in the Carrara marble. They are small, barely dents. Mary "appears disturbingly adolescent" and "underage for motherhood."[1] Art critics I've read point to various sources that may have influenced the young artist to minimize visible pain in the two polished forms: neo-platonic ideals popular in the day, poetic scenes from Dante's contemporary *Divine Comedy*, and the artist's own early convictions about Jesus and Mary and the theological messages their bodies should convey. "Michelangelo realized a work of absolute perfection that mirrors Divinity in the beauty of Christ's body and of the Virgin's face," Eugene Muntz writes. "[Mary] is sad yet seems reconciled with her lot."[2]

Michelangelo should have talked to his mother. She would have known better.

The four fingers on Mary's left hand, broken during a move and restored, seem least honest of all, open and upraised in the gesture of a worshipper in surrender. But the bow of her neck, the droop of her head, the helpless hand fallen to the side, the knees loose, having given up their attempt to cradle the much too large man-child were the same as that other suffering mother I visited one morning, knees slack and fallen wide, in the emergency room.

---

1. Eugène Müntz, *Michelangelo* (Parkstone International, 2012), 63. E-book accessed via Hoopla, June 8, 2021.

2. Muntz, *Michelangelo*, 63.

Organic Donor

He wanted to be an organ donor.

So I sat with his parents through
the excruciating phone call.
We'd left his blue and bloated body
at the hospital, a smear of holy oil on his forehead.

Now here, around the kitchen table
we discuss that body's twenty-two-year-old parts:
heart valves, eye lenses,
bones, tendons, skin,
the parts of a drug addict deemed useful
to a wider society
still battling its injuries and diseases
unlike this until-lately child
stone-still on the hospital gurney
blood dried and crusted in the corner
of his open mouth.
His fight is over.
His body bound and burdened no longer
    by the quick, hot high.
With flickering hope for the one hundred and fifty
    he could potentially help,
we endure the painful questions about needle use,
sexual habits, illegal escapes of choice,
past incarcerations
(the answer is ten days).

Forty-seven minutes later the final word is:
Thank You.
But I'm Sorry.
Behind bars more than seventy-two hours,
This body is disqualified.

And the mother who bore its fragile, emerging frame
within, later upon, her own,
who poured out blood, water, and milk
to build a growing bundle of valves,
lenses, bone, and skin
not so very long ago,
who cradled his infant form in her arms to nurse him,
closes her eyes to speak:

    "They can't use it."

    "They can't use any of it."

Blessing of the Orchard

In my experience the young die in spring.

It was a Tuesday in April, and I was already running late after some desperate exercise. I showered and hurriedly tried to nurse my baby. Still half-dressed when the phone buzzed, I assumed it was the secretary calling in veiled judgment at my delay. It was instead the last person I expected to call with an emergency. Her message was short.

"Please come. Our son died last night."

Please, come.

There's a father in John 4 who similarly pleads: "Lord, come before my son dies."

Jesus heads off on a tangent in response: "Unless you see miraculous signs and wonders, you won't believe."[1]

But this father isn't interested in a theological debate. He's single-minded. He hasn't got time for what millennials hate about the synagogue in Galilee. His kid is dying.

Please, come.

Jesus corrects course, realizes the official isn't there for show or good press or a photo op: "Go home," he answers. "Your son lives."

When I finally arrived at the hospital, I had no such reassurance for Matthew's mom. At age twenty-two, he was gone.

I sat with the family that day, first at the hospital and later in their home, praying silent strength beneath their phone calls, taking a break to express milk and tears together for my own infant son at home. The stories spilled out, stories of invisible burdens we never guess others carry, tales of what a mother will do to protect her son at least from the dangers of hitchhiking to his dealer through the night. That spring, I'd had multiple parents in my office, each suffering unseen terrors and trials due to young adult opioid addiction. It was 2011, before they started calling it an epidemic. Back then,

---

1. John 4:46–54 (CEB).

it was still someone's "poor choices" or "personal demons he tried and failed to defeat." We planned the church and cemetery services unaware that dozens of friends would swarm the graveside with yellow roses, pant legs pushed up to show fresh tattoos, raw grief written on their skin.

It was on that slow drive in the hearse between church and graveside that a funeral home director began my education in tissue donation, the giving away of our bodies for good. So sacred is the body in Indigenous spirituality that Native Americans don't usually donate their organs at all because of the deep connection between the body and the earth. Between the viewings inherited from Europe and the introduction of the peculiarly American practice of embalming, our death rituals can feel barbaric. Most of the time, our rituals and practices of death serve to distance friends and family from their loved one's body.

"You cannot look past what the job is," says one of my childhood friends who now works in tissue procurement. "Most of our donors are young." That means he and his employees have their hands in dead bodies every day. They see a lot of trauma. Sometimes, they also get to see a body restored or saved when a wounded veteran or other tissue recipient gets some of their life, health, or ability restored.

Nine months after his death, Matthew's family invited me to bless and dedicate a new orchard in their son's memory right around his birthday. It was in December, when so many families are setting out on mantles and beneath evergreen trees tiny mangers made of wood, cradles ready to receive a Christ child.

Bundled against the bitter Midwest winter wind, I recited a borrowed blessing over the orchard:

"Planting a Tree"[2]

Firm in this good brown earth
Set we our little tree
Cool dews will freshen it

---

2. Nancy Byrd Turner, "Planting a Tree," *Just for Fun* (Rand McNally & Co., 1939).

Summer showers will feed it
Sun will be warming it
As warmth is needed
Wind will blow round it freely
Take root, good tree!

Slowing, as the days go on,
These boughs will stouter be
Leaves will unfurl on thee,
And when Spring comes to you
Birds may build there,
Shade outstretch, wide and free—
Grow well, good tree!
In this good, brown earth.

I gave the littlest ones a bucket of water to sprinkle as we trooped to each bush or shrub to baptize and encourage it with the refrain "Take root, good tree!"

After the orchard blessing, I was invited along with my own spouse and kids to eat soup and join in the family Christmas cookie–making party inside. On our way back to the house, the boy's father showed us his new garden shed set in a limestone island. My son, toddling top-heavy at eighteen months, squatted down to drag his chubby fingers closed around fistfuls of limestone, his impulse toward ground, toward stone, toward earth since birth. More satisfying than two rocks in the palm, though, are two stones flying past a bush. He has been a thrower since the day he realized that his pitch and aim could fend off the sister twice his height from beyond her arm's reach.

He tossed a handful. By the time the second handful went airborne, our garden guide's hand was on his shoulder, a little too firmly. "No."

Not verbal yet, my curly-haired boy looked up at a man he did not know with unsure eyes that struggled to read the unfamiliar anger. He looked back at his own hand and slowly, reluctantly, uncurled his fingers, letting the rocks fall.

My heart caught for a moment watching my own child and won-
dering, as every parent does, whether this was a moment to shield or
protect or intervene, whether I had power enough to prevent even a
little of the bruising this world will wage against his body, mind, and
spirit. My son toddled near me, a bundle of my tender inner flesh
now walking around, destined for God-only-knows what scrapes and
breaks and wounds in the years to come. The two parents who had
welcomed us into their garden had suffered the worst. They would
never see their son in flesh again. I moved toward my own and took
his hand in reassurance—for him or for me or maybe for us both. I'm
here. I'm at your side.

I could hold him, for a time. I could not prevent whatever
might come.

The blueberry bushes we blessed that day died. Floods came the
following spring that filled fields with puddles for days, and blueberries "don't like to get their feet wet."

"We moved some. We'll replace the others when it dries out,"
the mother told me months later as we tackled opposite sides of a
berry bush on a pick-your-own farm. Our arms encircled the bushes
this time, and we worked outside with the sun and the sweat and
the bugs, not the alcohol-swabbed chrome and white sheets of the
emergency room. But it was still his body on the table between us, a
gurney altar-ed to join us across time.

It was from her that I learned the pastoral power of a blueberry
patch. It's not the blueberries, bulging toward dusty blueness in the
sun, but the fingers that find them and roll them loose to fall, gently,
into the bucket below. Those fingers and the brows they wipe beneath
straw hats, the sun already higher than you'd hoped by the time your
car makes its dusty way down the gravel lane to the farm and its field.
It was easier there, with the green branches between us, and the sun
and the sweat, to trade stories of grandparents and parents and children, to laugh at family, to ease into the question, "How are you and
God lately?" with a big blueberry held on the tongue, waiting to burst
its juice like a blanket of sweetness over the bitter, holding something
good, even if it is small and blue and smashable in the palm. Holding it
just gently enough, like a mother holds her son.

II: FOOD

In Plenty and In Want

A quality retreat distinguishes itself from the rest when the fare on the table is as colorful and rich as the company gathered around it. I confess to passing judgment as soon as I see the refreshment table at check-in. Is it ten aluminum cans of cola in a line? Are there fixings for frothy mugs of hot cocoa or good cream and sugar for your Earl Grey? I can't be the only one who goes on retreat for the good eating, whose favorite places on earth stand out in large part because of the food I ate there. From the small rounds of homemade honey wheat bread baked by the Sisters of St. Joseph a couple hours north of Minneapolis, Minnesota, to their sisters in Rocky River, Ohio, who spike the coffee with cinnamon and keep it fresh and hot all afternoon, wise hosts know that the heavenly banquet spread Jesus described needs to nourish more than a disembodied soul.

Taste and see, the Psalmist sings, how the word of God can come to us while we are cleaning our plate.

Before we moved out West, I received the birthday gift of a week-long workshop with other writers on Whidbey Island outside of Seattle, which also gave me a chance to visit a far-flung sibling nearby. It had been a very rough year financially and vocationally, and I could not believe my good luck as I arrived at the cabins tucked among the giant trees of the temperate rainforest we know as the Northern Cascades.

At the very first gathering, our workshop leader tried to head me off: "Don't waste time feeling insecure."

Don't waste time.

Don't waste.

Despite her warning, I did feel insecure. I felt undeserving—not embarrassed, but self-conscious. Like some kind of Cinderella poseur in a gown I feared might disappear, I trudged each morning through the Chinook woods to breakfast, where I tried to choose between ten tins of assorted organic teas.

One night they served vegan almond cheesecake for dessert, the smoothest, silky, rich coconut subbing for cream and cheese. Easy on my guts. I think I told a tablemate it was the food of the gods, intending no hyperbole at all.

Every lunch, they served nearly twenty avocadoes, halved on a plate. You could have a whole one all to yourself, if you wanted. Avocado. On the hill where I grew up in Ohio, that's rich-people food, or at least fare fit for Californians, which my childhood self figured was mostly the same thing.

In the Pacific Northwest, where I never imagined I'd live, Himalayan pink salt was all the rage. I had never seen it in a table shaker before. I sprinkled a little on my eggs. I tried not to overfill my plate.

Don't waste.

It was a common refrain in my childhood home.

Even on the Wednesday afternoons when I opened kitchen cupboards alone while Mom was still at work, I thought, "I'm hungry. What is there to eat?" Two and a half broken pieces of whole wheat lasagna noodles banged around in their box, long before anyone thought to make whole wheat pasta taste good. On the bottom shelf I found a half sleeve of generic white crackers and a jar of peanut butter. There was a packet of taco seasoning but nothing to put it on.

She would go shopping later, I would remind myself. After five o'clock that evening, when the banks are closed, her check could float through the night on the promise of the pay she would deposit the following day on her lunch break. Tonight, there would be food. But later.

Don't waste.

I grabbed the crackers and nut butter and a knife and made my plate.

Twice a month, on grocery shopping days, I overate, especially the treats. Our roller coaster seasons of scarcity timed poorly with my body's rounding tumble through puberty. Little yogurt packs, low-fat cookies, or sometimes cereal bars: I'd take three at a time from the shelves, tuck them under my sweatshirt, and sneak to my room. The cupboards were full. But tomorrow? Who knew?

Don't waste time.

It took me a decade or two to understand that the bodily scarcity I'd experienced in childhood rewired my neural pathways so that I almost cannot help but measure my place at sumptuously spread tables like those in the Chinook forest by the quality of the textile used to make my tablemate's scarf. I worried my gape-mouthed indecision at the breakfast buffet betrayed how little I belonged there. Food is the great equalizer, some say. Everyone eats. But I don't know. I've had plenty, and I've had want.

The week on Whidbey Island immersed me in a culture of plenty. Three times daily a wholesome and delicious meal was spread with an abundance my childhood never let me imagine. But just nine months before the avocado-enriched week I spent there, we had been in desperate want. I had made the calculation that if I did not find work soon, my children would qualify for free or reduced lunch at their elementary school. Like I did.

In seventh and eighth grade, when my mother supported four children on her own, and before the child support settlement came through, my name was on the list at the cashier's table in the converted gymnasium of my middle school. Already on a scholarship, I wasn't exactly conscious of the financial indignity. What I knew was that the food on those trays wasn't good. Pizza like cardboard smeared with tomato and cold cheese. Too-sweet apple puree.

We may feign innocence at the ways humans use food to control themselves and others. If you're good, you can have a candy. Are "deserving" and "dessert" related? Americans entangle the Latin and French roots on the regular, but maybe there's more to it than simply sloppy spelling. The twelve-year-old deep inside me still cannot be sure one does not mean the other—if not etymologically, then at least psychologically.

We are even miserly in church, cubing one-square-inch pieces of white bread for communion and calling it a feast.

Food.

Feel the shape of the word in your mouth. Food.

You have to take a bite to say it, have to put teeth to lower lip. Reading Thich Nhat Hanh's bite-sized *How to Eat*, I remember another place where God met me and grew me through the food on my plate. In a sunlit cafeteria on the edge of a Florida marsh, a priest once helped me and a group of clergy colleagues eat a mindful lunch. Like many helping professionals and caregivers, we can easily forget how to feed ourselves.

We started silently, just looking at the plates, which seemed to hold not much: ten garbanzo beans, a sliced beet, half a hard-boiled egg, some seeds, julienned peppers, grated carrots, and deep greens, arranged on a plate with an edible orchid, curling purple and white, from the center like a palette bejeweled.

We uncovered it, drank deeply of each color, noticed each vegetable and seed, inhaled the aroma—the smells of living things. Only after looking fully and smelling deeply did we choose one thing. Just one thing.

Beet.

Bean.

A snap.

A crunch.

Juice.

Sweet tang.

We put that one thing into our mouths, took one bite, and chewed slowly, letting all the flavor blend with the saliva on our tongue behind our teeth. We put our forks down so as not to rush for the efficiency of mechanics.

We chewed and swallowed that one bite.

Then we paused to give thanks.

I've never eaten so little and felt so full, so nourished, and so at peace.

We in North America put so much into our mouths without thinking, and often for reasons other than true hunger or thirst. It took an eating plan during Lent not long ago to help me regain some consciousness of how I was putting things in my mouth in the evening not out of delight or joy, but out of stress, worry, and fear.

When it came time to preach Jesus feeding the five thousand—the only miracle that appears in all four Gospels—I decided to get the story out of my head and into my hands. I decided to make bread. I decided to make bread from *Laurel's Kitchen*, the hippie natural foods bible of the 1970s that all my parents' friends used. I wanted to do it the way my mother had done it the first eleven years of my life when we lived up on that hill in the middle of nowhere, off the grid, growing our own food, and buying what we couldn't grow at a family friend's farm down the road. She baked the kind of bread that pretty much takes all day, with active dry yeast (not "rapid-rise") and stone-ground whole wheat flour. There was no bread machine. Her technology was the ceramic bread hook on her electric stand mixer.

The day before preaching the miraculous feeding story, I made a loaf of bread. Two, actually. And it took all day. And the first yeast I'd bought had lost its rising power, so I had to make a run to the store for more. In the evening rush of parenting and sermonating, I didn't get the rest and fold quite right, so something weird happened with the final proof that made my loaves look like they had boils. The bread was denser than I would have liked. A little heavy. Probably too much flour. I'm not sure the recipe was the easiest to follow, or that my mother's bread was ever that good. I know I missed it when, in the late '80s, our circumstances changed drastically, and we plunged into the reality of being latchkey kids who ate store-bought food, sustained by a struggling single mother.

It was in the 1980s that food banks really took off. Sara Miles writes that they were, at first, a start-up, activist response to what was perceived as an emergency affecting those who were homeless: "But hunger had persisted, becoming entrenched among the working poor—even as cheap fast-food proliferated and millions of pounds of fruit and vegetables kept getting plowed into landfills each year."[1] Food banks are better than many alternatives. They give people choice, which offers dignity. But they are, in some ways, a compromise with an economic system that just refuses to prioritize a living wage and the ability for every person to truly eat the fruit of their labor. Miles writes:

It was the abundance of American agriculture and the vast excess of the food system that made the work of the food banks

---

1. Sara Miles, *Take This Bread: A Radical Conversion* (New York: Ballantine Books, 2008), 104.

possible. . . . U.S. agricultural policy allowed farmers to hold
their product off the market to support price, meaning that when
production increased, farmers could plow food under or feed it by
the truckload to cattle instead of putting it on the market. This
excess food—along with any fruits and vegetables that didn't meet
the criteria for the perfect, unblemished, and standard-sized pro-
duce retailers wanted—was gleaned by the food banks.[2]

Food banks my mother remains proud today she never used.

What Sara Miles liked best about Jesus was that he called himself food. The former New York cook and Nicaraguan war correspon-
dent got to know this Jesus by way of the Eucharist at St. Gregory's
Episcopal Church in San Francisco, a story she tells in her memoir
Take This Bread, which is about her early exuberance in starting a
food pantry while wrestling with the politics of both church and food
and her own ego. Miles writes that she appreciated the way Jesus
associated with all the wrong people and told people not to be afraid:
"I liked all that, but mostly I liked that he said he was bread and told
his friends to eat him."[3]

It's this experience of Jesus as food, of being handed a loaf of
bread Sunday after Sunday and getting to tear off a chunk, that converted Miles to the religion her parents had protected her from, that
then helped her realize you can't be a Christian alone.

That story of the magically multiplying loaves and fishes evokes
the Good Shepherd of Psalm 23 to some storytellers. To others, it's
an ethic of abundance lived out hand to hand. To the storyteller we
call John, it's also a sign. John is big into signs. For him, this meal
is another sign to us about the nature and character of the "I AM"
presence that appeared to Moses in the bush, a sign that this Jesus is
connected to the same source as Moses, whose prayers shook loose
manna from heaven. Manna, that mysterious matter of nourishment, strange enough to the people they called it, "What is this?"
Jesus says, "I AM the bread of Life."

---

2. Miles, *Take This Bread*, 104.
3. Miles, *Take This Bread*, 92.

In John's version of this story, once they had their fill of that giant picnic and realized something even bigger was on offer, the people said, "Sir, give us this bread always."

There is a boldness to their request. They don't waste time feeling insecure. In one way they remind me of the thin orphan in the musical *Oliver!* who draws a short but eventually lucky straw. Or maybe the crowd reminds me of myself in those moments I still marvel at feeling full and satisfied.

A person who has been previously deprived and then finds themselves filled with food of the deeply nourishing kind, the kind that brings life to the body through color, flavor, and nutrient value alike, will extend their hands to ask, "Please, may I have some more?"

Give us this bread always.

Full

I t is rare to find a woman who hasn't danced with some form of eating disorder or body dysmorphia. We can feel the pain and hurt embedded deep in our flesh, but we may have trouble locating exactly where it resides. Invisible to the unaided eye—sometimes it takes a spiritual MRI—the wounds make their presence known.

My own dissociation with my body appeared, unsurprisingly, in my teen years.

I signed up for an anatomy and physiology course at the local college thanks to a deal that allowed high school seniors to take college courses. I was fascinated by the body. I wrote a research paper on multiple sclerosis in awe of the invisible ganglion. At the same time, I starved and purged and overexercised. These things feel dangerous to write about. Capitalism's entangled culture of consumption and distorted body image has oppressed so many people. Though my preference was laxative pills, I sometimes covered with dietary regimes. For a time, I tried vegetarianism but not for the ethics. "I don't digest meat well," I'd tell friends and family. And I held that line steadfastly for a decade more, even after I met, fell in love with, and married the man whose college housemates nicknamed him Meat Boy.

It is a sweet story. At that time, Adam and I did not attend the same school, but he lived in one of those campus-adjacent houses that lodged students no longer required to pay for campus residency, food, and board. Everyone just called it The House. A couple of unrelated Protestant campus ministers provided adult supervision to the motley collection of students living there who were mostly affiliated with the "artsy" campus ministry that met late on Thursday nights. I noticed the curly-haired guy who covered a Blues Traveler song with the band, but I mostly had only talked with and hung out with the women from that place. I had noticed him but did not know whether he had noticed me until the Thursday night he said, "Why don't you let me make you dinner sometime?"

"Okay." It was not hard to accept.

I was practiced at keeping myself alive by consuming enough calories. More than once, I had made a cold block of tofu cut from its vacuum-sealed, waxed-cardboard packaging and slipped into a bowl sufficient enough for that task. But I had never been good at feeding myself.

Meat Boy had only recently discovered he loved to cook. He had not learned how in his childhood, but he was spreading his wings in the house full of hippie Jesus vegetarians who had the Mennonite camp cookbook *More with Less* practically memorized. He started with the premise that half a pound of meat was a good beginning for making any meal.

When I arrived early one Thursday night and wedged myself into a chair at the table tucked in a kitchen nook, I didn't realize how much care he had invested in the simple pot of whole wheat spaghetti noodles and meatless marinara sauce. He ground the pepper and even grated his Parmesan cheese. We talked and talked. One of the women housemates I knew best came rushing through the kitchen but then slowed and stopped when she saw the scene. Eyebrows arched, she looked at me, then at him, then back at me, trying to figure out what was going on.

What was going on was more than just consuming calories. It was true food. Real nourishment. Our religious stories offer it repeatedly, but even as I sat at the table watching him cook, I doubted deep within that I deserved this gift of attention. Only after I met this man whose pick-up line was an offer to make me dinner did I begin to gradually and gratefully receive what my body most hungered for: adoration. The lifesaving nourishment of essential worth.

Body Scan

Begin at the feet, which don't touch the ground.
Feel the air current beneath, the ankles start to swell.
Notice the pain of that bunion and the ache of high arches.
Calves feeling puffy and the back of the knees sore.
A throb and a shiver grip the back of the right hamstring before
breaking into a bona fide pain in the ass where glute and piriformis
and obturator internus bind together beneath and across that ball
joint where femur butts its head into pelvic cradle.
From iliac crest to tip of sacrum, the whole thing feels liable to
disintegrate at any moment, collapse inward, pulverized by the
weight of bearing life,
then
now
In the belly, intestines scold with bloat inflated by a lunch full
of all the wrong foods.
Lumbar vertebrae crackle and pinch, stretched taut when pivoted
toward the window.
Shoulder blades "hike!" and "hut!" on either side of the spine,
prepared to tackle an opponent between, brace for impact.
This neck slips drunkenly around the compass directions, a lead
disk cinched
by a steel bandanna just above the brow line.
The top of the head itches,
a lid waiting to be flipped open
to be freed.

Listen to Your Gut

Runners will run for any of the body's ailing parts—especially to earn a free T-shirt. Collectively, each summer Americans race to cure them all: diabetes, pancreatic cancer, breast cancer, colon cancer. I am unsure how much progress we make.

Someone I love once ran a race sponsored by the Colon Cancer Coalition, and among the usual entertainments at the finish line sat a giant section of the human colon complete with malignant polyps and Crohn's ulcers crafted of foam, red netting, and paint. Walking through the ten-by-ten-foot, 150-pound excretory tunnel was supposed to entice people to schedule that colonoscopy.

I have no data on whether the strategy worked. The giant inflatable colon made headlines, though, when it was stolen from a driveway in Missouri in October 2018: it was mentioned online almost a thousand times and gave birth to the #StolenColon hashtag that was shared more than 6,500 times on Twitter.

Medical technology and pharmaceutical companies raised funds for two replacements before the sponsoring organization announced, with relief, the stolen colon had been found in an abandoned house. In the end, everything came out okay. If you only knew the puns I am withholding.

My family may be more obsessed with our gastrointestinal systems than most since my paternal grandfather died from advanced colon cancer, which was already Stage 4 when doctors discovered it. His bedtime snack of two dried prunes was our only clue. He liked his Beech-Nut chewing tobacco, so there is that. Our gut consciousness may go deeper than drawing tobacco juice and spitting, however.

So much neurological function occurs within its folds that the human intestinal track could be a second brain. When a friend first tried to convince me of this, I rolled my eyes. Given not only my grandfather's, but my father's and my own digestive history, though, I had to look it up.

I found the human gut is lined with more than one hundred million nerve cells.[1] I may have learned in grade school that the digestive tract releases hormone signals into the bloodstream, sending messages about fullness or hunger to the brain with a roughly ten-minute lag time. But more recent research shows the intestines have a direct line to the vagus nerve through a neural circuit that can send information in seconds. A few feet distant from the brain at most, my gut apparently has its own Wi-Fi. For decades now, I am afraid it too often flashed the warning, "Your Connection is Unstable."

Lactose is one of the usual suspects blamed for bloating and digestive issues, and intolerance for it does run in the family. In college, I heard some people didn't have enough acid to digest meat, so I thought that might be it. I turned vegetarian. My fasting, purging, and exercising routine made me feel lighter, empty, free. Running did seem to relax and move along whatever packed my bowels, so I ran more frequently. Still, in my early twenties, the pain periodically became so intense I would double over and cry in the bathroom, leave parties early, fall on hands and knees on the floor at home just trying to breathe until the bubbles moved. The one doctor I tried to see for help—a man—looked at me from across the room as if I was mentally unstable, told me to "eat more fiber, fruits, and vegetables," and prescribed a pill commonly used for irritable bowel syndrome without recording an actual diagnosis on my chart. He then rushed off late to his Thursday afternoon golf game. At the "more fiber" line, I pointed out that I was a vegetarian. He just shrugged his shoulders. Later, I was grateful he had not recorded a diagnosis because IBS is one of those "pre-existing conditions" for which I could have been denied the health insurance that for a time I went without.

During my first pregnancy, my vegetarianism went out the window. I craved large quantities of dairy milk and red meat. During the

---

1. Emily Underwood, "Your Gut Is Directly Connected to Your Brain, by a Newly Discovered Neuron Circuit," *Science*, September 20, 2018, *www.sciencemag.org/news/2018/09/your-gut-directly-connected-your-brain-newly-discovered-neuron-circuit#:~:text=FULLER%2FScience%20Source-,Your%20gut%20is%20directly%20connected%20to%20your%20brain,a%20newly%20discovered%20neuron%20circuit&text=The%20human%20gut%20is%20lined,practically%20a%20brain%20unto%20itself.*

second, I lost the ability to digest dairy and developed a sensitivity to soy so acute I could tell within two bites if it was mixed in the instant oatmeal commonly sold at coffee shops.

With the last of my pregnancies nearly a decade past, I could not understand why the bloating situation once again became so chronic as age forty drew near. For days at a time my belly looked five months pregnant if I didn't consciously suck it in. The cramping grew worse. Was it poor mental health this time?

What was my second brain trying to tell me?

Having long ago decided not to keep a bathroom scale in the house, and skittish about anything approximating a diet due to that nineteen-year-old purge-and-fast pattern described earlier, I nevertheless signed up one Lent to try a wellness program that eliminated common digestive offenders—dairy, gluten, alcohol, and sugar—before gradually adding them back to monitor the body's reaction. I wanted to pay attention to what I was consuming and why, to tune into true health.

The bloating disappeared. For four weeks, I felt great and slept better than I had in a long time, even though I really craved dessert. In reintroducing foods, there was one clear offender that made my gut revolt and blow up once again like a balloon: wheat bread.

Bread. That brown, dense, sweet staple of life. I could have lived on homemade whole wheat bread. I thought. Somewhere along the way, I had developed a sensitivity to gluten, that protein found in wheat, barley, and rye that knits together so well the strings and strands that bond under the heel of my kneading hands, pushing and pulling as instructed by Laurel writing in her kitchen. Maybe I'd always had it. Maybe that's why I could never drink more than one beer because it made me feel bloated or preferred the oat stouts to the wheat brews. Maybe that's why even vegetarianism didn't cure the pains that attacked my gut.

One of my dormmates in college lived with celiac disease but would occasionally eat what she knew she should not have, even though it made her sick. Pizza. Beer. It was college. I'm not sure it would have been possible to live on a campus in Ohio in the late 1990s without consuming gluten. I had a challenging enough time avoiding meat. She ate what she shouldn't even though she knew it would hurt.

Celiac disease is an autoimmune dysfunction in which gluten triggers an immune system attack on the small intestine. It's usually genetic, but it can develop at any age. The human body can be incredibly powerful fighting off a perceived attack, and celiac disease triggers chemical warfare against those delicately microscopic villi that line the small intestine like tiny fingers, multiplying the surface area to better absorb nutrients. Celiac disease attacks those villi with the body's own immune system, burning them down to stumps that cannot properly absorb what the body needs. Friendly fire. With acid. Even crumbs from a contaminated cutting board can cause damage.

My woes may not be full-blown celiac disease, which can be identified by a blood test, though I am increasingly intolerant. The chef in our house needed some convincing, but out of sympathy for the frequent attack of the five-month-gas-baby bloat, he even started storing my butter separate from the rest. All of this sure makes communion difficult. What happens when a Christian pastor can't digest Jesus?

Some of my childhood friends and relations have conducted their own kind of religious elimination diet and realized they cannot. They have converted to Judaism or Buddhism or have found agnosticism a more honest place for themselves.

Even in Jesus's day, quite a few could not stomach what he offered. Among what I call The Weirder Sayings of Jesus comes this one from the Gospel According to John, a discourse that follows the miraculous feeding of five thousand. I wonder if the disciples thought about trying to stop Jesus while he was still ahead with his satiated picnic guests and manna metaphors. Nevertheless, Jesus keeps going: "Very truly, I tell you, unless you eat the flesh of the Son of Man and drink his blood, you have no life in you. Those who eat my flesh and drink my blood have eternal life, and I will raise them up on the last day; for my flesh is true food and my blood is true drink."[2]

---

2. John 6:53–55.

I am still not entirely sure what he meant, even after a year of biblical Greek in graduate school. It doesn't seem "just metaphorical." Even among ancient audiences accustomed to startling rhetoric, Jesus's words do not sit well.

"This teaching is difficult," his disciples respond. "Who can accept it?"[3]

Our storyteller admits that some turned back and no longer followed him from this point on. From other sources we know these wild words even contributed to accusations of cannibalism.

Whether I am talking about food or faith, I am not going to win any evangelism awards for my advice: trust your gut. What makes you nauseous will not bring your body or your spirit health. This is one of my deepest convictions. Jesus never intended the Bread of Heaven to be force-fed. That is not what will give life to the world.

That said, I do make one request. Please check the label. Especially over the past fifty years, a whole lot marketed and sold under the Jesus brand has not been organic, if you will. Much of it is not even food. To carry the metaphor a bit further, it is more like texturized Jesus protein pretending to be what it is not. It will leave you malnourished or bloated even if you feel full. We check the lists of ingredients of the food we buy for allergens, chemicals, and other harmful products. Why should our spiritual food not be put to the same scrutiny?

Lest some toxic white nationalism, for example, pass undetected among "other natural flavors." Check those labels. Trust your gut.

---

3. John 6:60.

III: PLEASURE

My Uncle's Magazines

'm not sure I had the luxury of contemplating the body as a kid. Mindfulness, if introduced the way my elementary-aged children are learning it in school, would have been dismissed as some new age mumbo jumbo.

Where I came from, bodies were for working and for birthing. There was the occasional uncle who labored more mentally than physically—one on each side, a teacher and an engineer—but they were the oddity, the outliers. It's not as though farmers and carpenters don't use their brains. They do, all the time, and their calculations carry life-and-death consequences, but my family just didn't think about our bodies. We used them: to repair cars or motorcycles, maintain electrical or cable lines, fight fires, nurse the sick and aged, farm, garden, birth, nurse, organize and set up gun shows, build houses, milk cows, raise hogs, and drive school buses. There was only one place bodies were contemplated, gazed upon: the magazines in my uncle's closet.

I don't remember who was with me when we stumbled upon them. It might have been Thanksgiving or Christmas. We were playing hide-and-seek in the old farmhouse that various relatives took turns living in for periods at a time. On the floor of a closet under the eaves, we removed the top of a banking box to find full-colored photos of *Playboys* and *Playgirls* in all their '80s big hair, feathered bangs, and glory.

Most perplexing to me was the photo spread picturing two women lying on the floor, like yin and yang, each resting her head on the inside of the other's thigh, knees splayed, vagina in view, inches away from the tip of the other one's tongue.

"What is this?" I whispered aloud to no one. Whichever cousin was with me had lost interest or knew better than I did why those boxes could get us into trouble.

I flipped past the naked model on the stool, buttocks raised to the viewer, torso torqued to show large breasts hanging, too, within reach while she looked back over her right shoulder. She was white and blonde, her eyes stony.

Someone in the house desired gazing upon the human body, but the glossy magazine ones, not the emphysemic and barrel-waisted ones struggling with nicotine and hypertension and diabetes and cancer on the floors below.

I have been on the receiving end of gazes inflamed by desire. But desire alone is not necessarily holy.

There was that elder man who waited at the end of the greeting line after worship years ago, gripped my hand, and said, "I could listen to you all day." Still holding my hand and looking into my face, he waited a beat too long before he added, "I could look at you all day, too." Stunned, I dropped his hand while his wife just laughed next to him. "I have to keep him on a short leash," she said. Then he barked.

Desire can grow from a lot of different soils, which is why we need to work so hard to detangle the knotted intersections of power, violence, and history in our bodies. Objectification is not adoration.

The day three men walked six feet behind me for a block down Lee Road, catcalling, whistling, and stage-whisperingly appraising my backside, the codes of power and history made us more than just one woman and three men because my body is a white body. A white woman's body. And the three men behind me that day were Black. The safety of my white woman's body, or others like it, has been weaponized: police called, arrests made, Black men and boys killed for far less sexual harassment, even if only imagined. Those three men were adults, all taller and broader than I was. But even if they had been three high school students or three barely teens, my cells had already been preprogrammed to be afraid, to fear violence or death—even in the broad daylight—because of how I had been taught to look at their bodies and mine. Having tried and failed to let them pass me, I made it look like the public library lobby was where I was headed anyway. I took the steps not too fast and slipped behind the relative safety of those heavy glass doors, glancing back to make sure they continued past. I waited. Just to make sure, I browsed the display of holiday cookbooks near the checkout, even though I don't cook.

How do we find our footing on the slippery paths between fetishization, adoration, weaponization, and oppression? Healing our erotic life would surely help.

"There are many kinds of power, used and unused, acknowledged or otherwise," Audre Lorde begins her landmark essay "The Uses of the Erotic."[1] "The erotic is a resource within each of us that lies in a deeply female and spiritual plane, firmly rooted in the power of our unexpressed or unrecognized feeling. In order to perpetuate itself, every oppression must corrupt or distort those various sources of power within the culture of the oppressed that can provide energy for change."[2]

Religious folks especially confuse the pornographic and the erotic. The former is sensation without feeling. The latter "has often been misnamed by men and used against women,"[3] Lorde writes. It is the creative energy of deep feeling, shared, that can bridge the spiritual and the political dimensions so falsely opposed.

Creative, not consuming. The erotic provides power, reminds us of our capacity for joy, and, because it fulfills the deepest and most universal human needs, can connect people across similarities and differences.

An even partly restored erotic life could mend ancient fractures between soma and spirit. No wonder so many religious powers have feared it.

---

1. Audre Lorde, "The Uses of the Erotic," in *Sister Outsider: Essays and Speeches* (New York: Penguin Books, 2020), 41, first delivered at Mount Holyoke College, August 25, 1978.

2. Lorde, "The Uses of the Erotic," 41.

3. Lorde, "The Uses of the Erotic," 42.

First Crust

O
f all the sweet lists and sketches and memories she could have picked from among its pages, the very first question my newly tween daughter asked me to answer in the mother-daughter journal I gave for her birthday was, "Who was your first crush?"

Privately, I reviewed the nicknames a friend and I had created in best-friend secret code. I wrote about how he attracted me one summer at camp with his black hair cut close to his head, drew me in with his perfectly white-toothed grin and light brown skin. His eyes danced in a way that made me suspect that intelligence and interesting thoughts ran the lights and gears behind them. That's what I wrote in my mother-daughter journal these decades later, anyway.

It is possible he was just hot.

I can still see his tanned belly showing between the raw punk edge of his cut-off T-shirt and the waistband of his black jersey shorts. That year at summer camp, he wore that same outfit daily, its dingy white T-shirt emblazoned with the orange and brown logo of the Cleveland Browns. With mirrored *Top Gun* sunglasses, he'd lean over the railing of the second-floor balcony onto the sunny yards below, sidekicks Rob and Marc slung casually at either shoulder, lankier, much more pale, and not half as graceful.

He was a bronzed and black-eyed mystery.

It really was his body that attracted me in my eleven-year-old naivete. His body and the way he carried it, especially the way it all moved like a liquid pool, smoothly following the lead of that brilliant smile. A Tom Cruise smile, bright, shining, and impish. Suave, which is not an adjective I've ever used for a sixth grade boy since. When other kids that summer found out that I liked him, they were way more interested in the possibility of our mutual infatuation as a topic of conversation than I was. The fire I'd been tending privately, internally, began to flicker and turn to queasiness. With glee, one so-called friend relayed a prepubescent brainstorm they had cooked up in my absence: they were going to duct tape us together at the mouth.

Revolted and puzzled at why anyone would have thought that was titillating, I fled to a deserted stairwell and locked the door. They couldn't see me. I think I had spent all of my sobs by the time a real friend found me there, red-eyed. She was surprised but empathetic. She sat and listened and offered to call off the hormonal mob. I think it worked. I tried not to be noticed for the rest of the week.

I had entertained a fantasy that his strutting on the balcony had been for me, for my eyes. But I could have been wrong. He moved with his family for his father's new job not long after that. I wrote him a couple letters, presuming nothing more than friendship. He wrote a couple back, and I read them alone in the pop-up camper that perched on the top of our hill that summer, alone again with my private fire and free to imagine futures together that might yet be.

"How are you?" I'd write. "I'm okay. My dad is fixing a car this week."

Oh, the raptures of adolescent romance.

Our paths crossed unexpectedly years later. I ran into him when we both made unplanned visits to our old church. I had driven down to Columbus for some college internship or grad school interview, and he had come to his former home's neighborhood to roam old stomping grounds.

He'd gone a bit wild and converted to Catholicism—that's how we evangelical youth rebelled—and pierced his tongue. I asked him how he kept that metal stud from breaking his teeth, and he laughed with that life-loving smile beneath the same dancing eyes. Damn, he was still hot. We were both committed to others at the time, but that didn't keep my body from recognition.

When does a repressed, keep-it-covered daughter of Christian conservatism awaken to carnal desire? For years, I had told myself it didn't happen until college, when I wrote a few of these on the way home from a date:

sweet little somethings
like remembering the pleasure
of palming the flesh
above his knee

I cannot pinpoint one day or one specific moment, but somewhere between that sixth-grade summer camp romance and my first year of college I must have shut a lot down in the department of bodily appetites. As a teenager at the annual family reunion one August, I remember euphemistically narrating a story that two people had recently "done the nasty," meaning sexual intercourse.

My youngest aunt overheard and turned around.

"What makes you think it's nasty?"

To this day I am glad she asked. It took me years to puzzle out the answer and learn I was wrong. The truth is that any sex education in the religious and educational circles that shaped me limited itself to physiology, function, and fear: don't get pregnant. I did not realize pleasure was a possibility and even part of the design until I felt the warmth of another eighteen-year-old thigh against my own while watching a movie side by side on a couch. Increased blood flow, a heightened sensitivity in my skin, a flushed face. The magnetism of skin on skin. It felt good. I learned to kiss. I learned to give and—what is often harder—receive the joys of the flesh.

The body takes its own sweet time.

Vessel of Joy

ike most humans, sexuality had always been part of the whole me. In the most desperate times of early adulthood, it was the joys of the flesh that finally got me to the doctor. Or, rather, their noticeable absence.

"Of all the things going wrong in my life, that wasn't one of them," I told the doctor at the free and reduced-fee clinic where I'd landed—laid-off and with no medical insurance—for birth control and an antidepressant refill.

She looked me over thoughtfully, sizing up the severity of the suicidal ideation I'd just described to her. I learned the name for it from her medical chart and was less concerned with the ideation than the recent disappearance of that glorious "O" on the occasions I was feeling human enough to make love with my spouse. Inability to orgasm, she told me, was a not uncommon side effect of the medication I'd been prescribed to keep me from making even grander plans for jumping off the valley bridge.

"That's why I don't usually prescribe that one for young people," she said as she wrote a new scrip for a different one.

"Thank God," I thought. I may hate my life, but the sex had at least been good. It may have even saved me.

Ally

There was a time when I would have never picked up a copy of Sonya Renee Taylor's book *The Body Is Not an Apology* because it had the words "self-love" in the subtitle, and my religion had taught me that the "self" was corrupt and couldn't be trusted. "Self" was the diseased root that produced all the fruit of sin, pride, poor choices, and bad government. Also, the author posed completely naked on the cover, save for some strategically placed hydrangea blossoms.

A time came, though, when my body refused to do what I kept forcing it to do: absorb the blunt force of trauma both first- and secondhand, bury it, and push on unflinching, teeth gritted.

I have strong and stubborn teeth, small and square and tight together. Even their baby versions stayed rooted until middle school, one baby tooth even refusing to leave my mouth until pried out to make room for orthodontics in my thirties. My teeth resisted all cavities. Dentists mistakenly assumed I was the beneficiary of the chlorinated water municipalities started supplying to the children of more recent generations. But no.

"We lived in the country," I'd tell the new dentist, every time. "We had well water." They never knew what to say to that. They did repeatedly recommend bite plates, though.

The decades have etched stress fractures in my canines and incisors and molars. Slender hairlines every dentist warns could lead to early dentures without care and a bite guard, but I even bite through my bite plate–thickened retainer.

If I was old enough to be warned about early dentures, I decided I was old enough to be seen reading a book covered by Taylor joyfully wearing only her birthday suit. Her words invited me to set some of my teeth-cracking baggage down.

> When we speak of the ills of the world—violence, poverty, injustice—we are not speaking conceptually. We are talking about

54

things that happen to bodies. . . . A radical self-love world is a world free from the systems of oppression that make it difficult and sometimes deadly to live in our bodies.[1]

Finding that self-love takes the kind of unapologetic inquiry and radical reflection Taylor offers through her work, inquiry that moves from the inside out, from the self to the society, from the politicized body to the body politic, from the part to the whole.

"Relationships with our bodies are social, political, and economic inheritances," Taylor writes.[2] Religious inheritances, too. Whenever and wherever we've been taught to fear, control, and absorb abuse in these bodies, we've been acclimated and trained to fear, control, and accept the abuse of other bodies not our own. "What if we all became committed to the idea that no one should have to apologize for being a human in a body?" she asks.[3]

I don't believe the religion of Jesus divided body from spirit, split the self or the soul from the whole, the material from the spiritual, or condemned the carnal in ways centuries of Christians would go on to do. A rabbi notorious for hanging out with sex workers and people suffering from seeping communicable skin diseases clearly wasn't put off by body fluids. Jesus could pull a parable from the organic experiences of gastrointestinal digestion and defecation or make inside jokes about impotence and levirate marriage. Maybe the religion's first and loudest interpreter, the zealous Saul-turned-Paul, got a little hot and bothered by long-haired women—or, more likely, some local fertility cult he associated with long hair. But even at thirteen, I suspected Jesus didn't care whether the girls on my Christian middle school basketball cheerleading squad showed the skin of our knees.

I am not making that up. For all away games my eighth grade year, we wore white lace ankled tights beneath our blue and white cheer skirts. We called them "skins." They were designed to keep us

---

1. Sonya Renee Taylor, *The Body Is Not an Apology: The Power of Radical Self-Love* (Oakland, CA: Berrett-Koehler Publishers, 2018), 4.

2. Taylor, *The Body Is Not an Apology*, 37.

3. Taylor, *The Body Is Not an Apology*, 14.

from showing any. It also kept us from feeling the rush of air as two teams of sinewy adolescent boys leapt and flew down the court. My one-season foray into cheerleading was a short-lived experiment in identity. I liked the screaming and shouting part but preferred to feel the rushing air on my own skin.

I teach myself a little more each year how to enjoy the skin I am in and to honor how it feels.

Taylor's prescription is a lifestyle always in process of thinking, being, and doing. Toward the end of her book she offered mantras to try on for size. When I got to the one that caught in my throat, I knew it was mine: "My body is my ally."[4]

Just for kicks, I then tried to write one of my own, what I might say about my body if I were truly free from shame and violence: "My body is a vessel of joy."

---

4. Taylor, *The Body Is Not an Apology*, 102.

Hands Dripping with Myrrh

Sustain me with raisins,
refresh me with apples;
For I am faint with love.

—*Song of Songs 2:5*

Arise, my love, my fair one,
and come away;
for now the winter is past,
the rain is over and gone.
The flowers appear on the earth;
the time of singing has come,
And the voice of the turtledove
is heard in our land.

—*Song of Songs 2:10–12*

Skin on skin. Observant readers will find skin aplenty in the sacred writings of Judaism and Christianity. Biblical authors and poets wrestle with sexual health and sexual ethics, with what makes a family, with how bodies are fed and cleaned and sheltered—and whose. If we use Audre Lorde's definition of deep feeling, shared and capable of empowering change, there is also plenty of the erotic.

Song of Songs—sometimes called the Song of Solomon, that sensual classic of Hebrew scripture—is for many a spiritual work prescribed not erroneously for those struggling to pray. Prayer and sex are both practices of intimacy.[1] The Song is also a powerfully erotic poem. When I preach with it, there are passages too suggestive to

---

1. Eugene Peterson, *Five Smooth Stones for Pastoral Work* (Grand Rapids, MI: Eerdmans, 1992).

use in corporate worship without all of our minds wandering off into fantasy or having somewhere to excuse ourselves for privacy and a guaranteed babysitter after lunch. All those twin gazelles and young stags browsing among the lilies on the cleft of the mountain. All those fruit trees to climb, figs to sample, and blossoms putting forth their fragrance. Alabaster thighs. Hands thrusting through openings in doors, other hands and fingers dripping with myrrh.

See what I mean?

In Hebrew, this romping, suggestive ode to romantic love is titled "the most excellent of songs" and attributed to Solomon, even though the primary voice is a woman's. It celebrates physical beauty and romantic love unlike any other sacred scripture. Its first words—"Kiss me!"—are a direct and urgent appeal for erotic intimacy, but the song is not alone in acknowledging the erotic in human existence. There's a euphemism-laced story about Ruth the Moabite dolling herself up to approach Boaz during a tipsy harvest celebration that stretched into the night on the threshing floor, punctuated by her mother-in-law's instruction, "He will tell you what to do."[2] We know that Jonathon's love was to David "greater than that of women" and that they sealed their commitment to one another bodily, with a pledge involving their robes, hands, and thighs. After the exile and geopolitical and religious struggles that attended first Greek and then Roman occupation, Jesus did not show up on the scene all ascetic and unmoved by the passions, either. He lets a woman cry on his feet then wash and dry them with her long hair. In another story, the same or a different woman anoints his head with expensive spiced oil. She is there for a while. Long enough to make things awkward for the other dinner party guests, who resort to using the woman's erotic powers against her by questioning her reputation. Tell me there wasn't some "shared, deep feeling" in that exchange. The "disciple whom Jesus loved," whoever they were, has made a lot of money for the novelist Dan Brown and others who have speculated about whether Jesus ever coupled or had a secret child.

---

2. Ruth 3:4.

And yet, for nearly fifteen hundred years, this religion that has been carried by colonizers and evangelizers from Western Asia throughout the world taught its followers to suspect the body, to distrust the body, to blame the body for all the evil in the world, and, if necessary, to beat the longings and the passion out of it.

It might have all been otherwise.

If only there'd been a decent curriculum of comprehensive sexuality education for teenagers back in the fourth century. Alas, the sexual shame of sixteen-year-old boys can do a lot of damage. A whole lot. While Athanasius may have offered us the possibility of seeing every body as potentially divine—or at least capable of sharing some of Jesus's divinity—Augustine's ideas about good, bad, and bodies are what most shaped the European-descended Christianity I inherited.

It's a shame. Literally.

I've always felt a little sheepish that I could not myself read more than a page or two of Augustine's *Confessions*. Also that I judge this theological giant for his obvious mommy issues and for treating his partner of fourteen years (and the mother of his child) like dirt. Family systems theory hadn't been invented yet when sixteen-year-old Auggie got triangulated into his parents' strained marriage, so perhaps I'm not being fair. But apparently, an embarrassing adolescent experience that occurred while accompanying his father to the public bath triggered his mother, Monica, to become extraordinarily involved—even by ancient standards—in Augustine's faith, job, and sex life ever afterward. I'm sure his schoolmates called her "Smother" behind his back. Auggie headed off to college at Carthage, which in his narrative sounds a lot like a sex-obsessed college student's fantasy of Spring Break but year-round and without cars. He did finally settle down, sort of, with a woman with whom he had a child. We don't know her name. That's how well he treated her until sending her away at his mother's insistence so she couldn't interfere with Augustine's ascending career as philosopher and teacher and late-in-life monk. He and his mother had a rapturous conversation at a window one day, after which they concluded that "no bodily pleasure, no matter how great, could ever match the happiness of the saints."[3] As he narrated it around 397 CE, mother and son left matter behind for a moment and ascended toward the spiritual realm and eternity. Whoever translates this out of body experience from the original Latin, it is clear the pair shared some sort of transcendent rendezvous with God. "The mouth of our hearts opened wide to drink in those celestial streams of Your fountain, the fountain of life."[4] The scholar Stephen Greenblatt quotes from Sarah Ruden's quite colloquial translation published in 2017: "While we were speaking and panting for it, with a thrust that required all the heart's strength, we brushed against it slightly."[5]

It was a life-changing encounter for Augustine, and also a little weird to read today, what with the panting and thrusting and sighing afterward. With his mother.

What did this moment mean for us? Genuinely bothered by how much harm humans can cause, Augustine became obsessed with figuring out why. Why would he and his college bros destroy something good—a pear orchard for instance—for no good reason at all? The problem went deeper than simple lack of willpower. Without alternatives like "raging hormones" or "childhood trauma survival skills," Augustine seized upon a theological dilemma that would dog him for the rest of his life: sometimes erections happen when we really wish they would not.[6] Or, to paraphrase the contemporary philosopher Ani DiFranco, "you can't will your [vagina] wet."[7] Augustine was bothered by arousal, by how a human who can exercise free will in every other area cannot always control his penis. He decided the root of arousal was lust—he dubbed it concupiscence—and decided

---

3. Stephen Greenblatt, "How St. Augustine Invented Sex," *The New Yorker*, June 12, 2017, accessed January 15, 2021, *https://www.newyorker.com/magazine/2017/06/19/how-st-augustine-invented-sex*.

4. Augustine, *Confessions: A New Translation*, Book IX [10.23] trans. Peter Constantine (New York: Liveright Publishing Corporation / W.W. Norton & Co., 2018), 180.

5. Augustine, *Confessions*, Book IX [10.24] trans. Sarah Ruden (New York: The Modern Library/Penguin Random House LLC, 2017).

6. Augustine, *Confessions: A New Translation*, Book X [30.41] trans. Peter Constantine (New York: Liveright Publishing Corporation / W.W. Norton & Co., 2018), 219.

7. Ani DiFranco, "Callous," *Knuckle Down*, Righteous Babe Music / BMI, 2005.

it was the origin of what was fundamentally broken in human beings from conception. He became obsessed with the sex life of those mythical first parents of Genesis, Adam and Eve, and whether they could potentially have had sex without arousal before they disobeyed and sampled the fruit of that notorious tree. That those two felt shame when God came calling afterward and covered themselves Augustine cited as proof that the ardor or lust that animated human genitals wasn't part of how they were created, but rather "a touch of evil." His interpretation forever changed the story of Adam and Eve, writing between its lines the idea of original sin for centuries afterward.

We keep repeating Augustine's mistake. "Culture adopts a random act of biology and tries to make it Meaningful, with a capital 'Mmmh,'" the sexuality researcher and author Emily Nagoski writes. "We metaphorize genitals, seeing what they are like rather than what they are, we superimpose cultural Meaning on them."[8]

Religious meaning, too.

Take one of Nagoski's many examples: medieval anatomists called women's external genitals the "pudendum," which comes from the Latin for "to make ashamed," because they are tucked away as if they *want* to be hidden, whereas men's genitals hang out in front for all to see. Religion's conclusion: women's genitals are a source of shame. Science's conclusion: women have all the equivalent parts, differently arranged. They are smaller and internal not because they are shy or ashamed, but because they don't have to transport our DNA from inside our own bodies into the body of someone else.

Even without this scientific knowledge at hand, Augustine had plenty of critics. Contemporaries accused him of falling into popular heresies that denigrated the material world and elevated the spiritual. Then, as now, a lot of people believed humans beings were born innocent—blank slates who get the opportunity to choose the bad or the good. Infants do not enter the world with some innate stain upon their hearts. Besides, they pointed out, why would a holy God choose to become a human in Jesus if human bodies were so inherently evil?

---

8. Emily Nagoski, *Come as You Are: The Surprising New Science That Will Transform Your Sex Life* (New York: Simon & Schuster, 2015), 16–17.

I really wish these folks had won the day. Many a baptism and infant dedication would be that much more tolerable. I wouldn't risk spraining my eyes trying to keep them from rolling out of their sockets when pastors go on about the evil stain on the heart of the six-month-old infant who just spit up on his little satin vest.

Augustine responded by twisting the story of Jesus's birth, too. Rather than finding in the Virgin Birth an early Christian echo of the miracle birth stories of Sarah and Hannah—women of low regard who, after divine visitation, go on to birth liberators and leaders of their people—he decided that the Holy Spirit coming upon Mary meant Jesus was conceived without any lust at all and so missed out on the transfer of guilt. Never having had sex with a man still wasn't quite enough. Later theologians decided that if Jesus could tolerate being born from the "shamefaced" parts of a woman, then her flesh must have been unstained and guilt free, too. So, the "Immaculate Conception" is actually about Mary's parents getting it on to conceive her without, erm, any ardor being involved. You may have seen an icon depicting these two chastely holding hands and looking deeply into one another's eyes. That was the moment.

Absent these angelic interventions, the message for the rest of us became, "Screw, if you must, but know that you'll be damned if you do." Erasmus piled on. John Calvin, too. The apostle Paul, so shaped by Greco-Roman dualism between "the flesh and the spirit," did not help.

This is how we got where we are. Prayer is good. Sex is bad. Unless you can't control yourself, in which case it is at least better to get into a solid, monogamous, heterosexual marriage than to go down to the public baths and contract an STI. Any other theological idea that might promote respect, relationship, and responsibility got shoved to the margins. I'm convinced that the doctrine of original sin and the location of that stain in our erotic lives allowed an increasingly imperialistic religion to deaden itself to the deep feelings of connection that Audre Lorde describes as a power capable of affecting justice and change. It made us more comfortable with violence: the violence we do to our own bodies to keep them in line and the violence done to other bodies through the years in Jesus's name.

Despite all the other places in our religious story where the human body is caressed and cherished, anointed and kissed, blessed and called good, Nietzsche wasn't wrong when he wrote in *Beyond Good and Evil*, "Christianity gave Eros poison to drink."[9] Nietzsche was in his case personifying the deep shared feelings of pleasure, ardor, and desire as the masculine Greek god of romantic love.

"[Eros] did not die of it, it's true, but he deteriorated, into a vice."[10]

---

9. Friedrich Nietzsche, *Beyond Good and Evil*, IV: 168, trans. Marion Faber (New York: Oxford University Press, Inc., 1998, 2008), 71.

10. Nietzsche, *Beyond Good and Evil*, 71.

With My Body

Sam lay supine in the bedroom—not the family room, where we had chatted before of God and trust, honesty and betrayal. Weeks earlier, maybe months, he had exposed his agnosticism to me, confessed the limitations of this divine romance. He'd shown me his spiritual scars, shed tears of grief, and exposed without shame that mix of contempt, disgust, and heartbrokenness left in the unkempt bed of a cleric who mistook one lover for another, as his former pastor had done.

Displaced to the bedroom now, Sam lived beyond the place words can work. He breathed only, and that barely. The three women in his life and I encircled the bed to release him with love. The blessing I brought was bold: a sensual, hands-on ritual that I started, innocently enough, at his head.

"We thank you and your head for . . . the ways that you influenced our lives by your beliefs, attitudes, and values. Thank you for sharing your hopes and dreams. We especially thank you and your head for . . ." Everyone took their turn to speak some specific thing, and after each one we concluded in chorus, "You will always be part of our hearts. Go in peace."[1]

But as we worked our way down his body, past eyes and ears and mouth, shoulders and hands, moving toward his feet, I paused briefly above his groin. I hadn't practiced this part.

"We thank you and your . . . manhood . . . for the seed of life which you gave to your children. For making you a father and a lover. Your masculinity gave passion and color to your life. We thank you and . . . your manhood for . . ."

His soon-to-be widow did not flinch as I spoke thanks for the pleasure his body gave and received, for the powers of procreation

---

1. Joyce Rupp, "Blessing of One Who Draws Near to Death," in *Out of the Ordinary: Prayers, Poems, and Reflections for Every Season* (Notre Dame, IN: Ave Maria Press, 2000), 71–74.

and the two middle-aged daughters he helped bring into the world. She smiled from sexual memory and said, "You were always such a good kisser." Their grown daughters grinned through bitten lips and sticky tears.

I berated myself on the way home. "Manhood?"

What ridiculously repressed euphemism had I grasped? The truth is I'd balked at saying "sexual organs" in such a sacred time and place. That's what the nun of uncommon blessings had written in my book. I had skirted the issue, and it made me wonder if the word *sex* was so out of place in prayer? Would "genitals" have been easier to say out loud? Reproductive equipment? Lover's "junk"?

When I met with my first couple for premarriage preparations, just thirty days after my ordination, the bride and groom had asked to have all references to "physical union" edited out.

"We don't want anyone thinking about us having sex," they explained.

My spouse and I had not so demurred. We quoted passages from the Song of Songs to one another before our wedding vows. The pastor confided to us later that those sacred texts got our church friends so hot and bothered that they demanded he preach a couple sermons on sex.

But we were the exception, not the norm.

The old Anglican liturgy is startlingly forward: "With my body, I thee worship," though in 1549, only the man said it as he bestowed a golden ring on his bride's left hand. But long gone from any of my Protestant wedding liturgies is the consecration of the conjugal act, with its assumption that anyone present on that day might be launching some maiden carnal voyage. It leaves us wanting, at death's door, where the longing and the need has not diminished any more than the humanity of either the dearly departed or their bereaved.

Fred was killed on Valentine's Day. He had sent flowers to his wife's workplace the week before, expressing remorse for some small inconsiderate word or deed Barb honestly could not remember. They were spending the holiday quietly, snowbound in their empty nest perched a little way up a gravel road, their three beautiful birds grown and living in other cities.

As they snuggled in against the winter storms and ice coating highways, the phone rang. It was Barb's sister. Her car had slid on the icy state route; she was waiting for a tow. Everyone was okay. The fender was too badly bent to drive the car, and she needed a ride. It was the kind of thing he did, this man more tender toward his wife and girls than many I had buried.

"Be right back," he told his wife, throwing on his coat and boots.

A tow truck shortage meant they were not all clear of the road—not the sister-in-law, not the sheriff's deputy, not Fred. When an inebriated driver in an SUV topped the hill at a high speed, metal hit metal, then metal hit flesh, and then flesh hit ground.

Fred looked only shaken at first, maybe bruised; he picked himself up and dusted off. But somewhere en route to the hospital, supine in the ambulance, some small tripped-up cluster of cells in his heart or veins or brain just stopped. He was gone.

Fred's blessing was harder in a way. By the time the family and I encircled him, he was further from life than others like Sam, further still removed by the requisite coroner's investigation and days spent in the morgue. Still in shock when they were called to confirm his identity, the family had not been prepared to thank the body they identified. They wanted desperately to see him again, so, by some miracle of mortuary art, the funeral home director made possible one last goodbye.

Leaning into my past experience, I guided our hands through the air from body part to body part. I paused above the bloated lower trunk but not midsentence.

"We bless you and your sexual and reproductive organs and give thanks for the seed of life. . . . We thank you and your sexual organs for . . ."

An awkward silence followed, but the widow did give wail to her worship.

"You were my one and only," she sobbed.

IV: PAIN

Robin's Egg Blue

three robin's eggs
of that perfect hue
held softly in their woven bowl
in the crook of a windowsill
high against a second-floor bathroom
a gift whose image I hold softly
in my suspended palm
waiting in this sterile room
for some clue to the blue
small ovoid soft tissue density
nestled in the crook of an internal organ
where it shouldn't be
woven with its wall
inseparably

Noticing

Too few months after our big move, in a year when trauma piled on trauma without giving us any break, I received a text from Adam that he was driving himself to the emergency room. He undersold how bad he felt. He almost drove back home before trying to walk it out on the sidewalk where he nearly passed out from fever and severe abdominal pain. Tests, tests, and more tests. The day after our sleepless night, a nursing assistant on the phone tried to say "tumor board" as nonchalantly as if it were the "solid waste district" meeting to discuss the minutia of municipal drainpipe overflow and not whether my spouse of twenty years had cancer.

It was a puzzle, apparently: a growth local internists had never seen but only heard about. They referred us to the research university five hours north. After repeated scans, redos, and the inane bureaucratic fumbles involved in getting the right pictures using the right contrasts mailed to the right places, we finally got to see the experts, who narrowed it down to one of four varieties of choledochal cysts. Super rare: one in every 100,000 to 150,000 humans born in North America or Western Europe, four times more likely in females than males, and most common for someone who is East Asian or Japanese, which Adam was not. It had probably been growing there quietly since his birth. But it was an inch in diameter now and inflamed, which was not good. Though it was "probably not cancer," it could become cancer, which was why they recommended cutting it out. Also, it could be complicated depending on how much of the biliary ductwork, gall bladder, and liver organ tissue was involved. If any needed reconstruction, we were advised that we would want transplant surgeons wielding the knives.

We were eating breakfast before our drive to the surgeon's office when I flipped the sandwich plate upside down over a steaming mug of turmeric tea and read aloud what was printed on the bottom of the perfectly white ceramic: "Williams Sonoma Everyday Dinnerware."

I didn't say aloud what I thought: "As if everyday folks can afford Williams Sonoma dinnerware every day."

I did say aloud, "I can't help noticing these things. I wish I didn't notice them."

"Of course you notice them," Adam said, "It's what made you a good journalist. Whether you found the career because you're good at noticing, or whether the other way around . . ."

It was a day to notice things, I thought. We were due for our pre-op appointment in a little over two hours. The kids were safely ensconced with barely known acquaintances hundreds of miles away. A friend would drive them to us when. . . . Well, when we knew. In a rush, we were in the car, a limited number of minutes and miles between us and the doctor's office.

I did not notice that day so much as absorb impressions like waves: a rush of sounds in the doctor's office, the words "we might have to postpone," a quick pen drawing on my notepad, and a triangle retraced several times over.

"This is the piece of liver we might have to remove."

"Section" was the technical term.

The liver transplant surgeon cheerfully reminded me that the liver was the only internal organ humans can regrow if some or even half needed to be cut out.

"Worst case scenario," he said, "we have to remove 20 percent." We walked, and then we rode the cable car down from the hospital on the hill, floating, time out of time; then we waited, contemplating broth in a plastic noodle bowl from the food cart.

The day between pre-op and surgery has disappeared from memory; it has become a trail I can trace only through snapshots posted on social media.

On the big day—they day they were to cut—I noticed too much in the predawn. I noticed how pale and vulnerable my husband's skin looked after he removed his regular clothes, and I helped him wipe down his hairy back and belly with the provided packets of antibacterial napkins. His skin was tinged green—whether due to the surgical prep room's neon lights or the unwanted cyst pooling bile in his gut, I couldn't say. Robed finally in a washed-out blue hospital gown, he settled into the wheeled bed. Once the professionals crowded around, I noticed how the anesthesiology resident tapped the IV ports repeatedly as he referred to them, and I winced each time. A bit thickset, with bushy brown hair, he recited as if reading an invisible flash card. His supervisor, a short woman with a smooth bob, covered with a patterned hair kerchief of Caribbean blue, leaned across my love's body possessively to address the OR prep nurse with a slightly frozen smile.

"I have a favor to ask," she said. "Save the antecubital fossa/vena basilica for me, please?"

The OR nurse looked pissed, but he contained it. "Sure thing." They were running behind. He unknotted the rubber tubing above the elbow in one deft pass of his hand. "Done."

A voice over the presurgical department speaker chided everyone with the announcement it is now twenty minutes past seven as the OR nurse knelt anew above the backside of the patient's right hand. My husband is a notoriously "hard stick." At the sight of a needle his veins seem to actually shrink, hike up their cells, and disappear, the vascular version of a "no thank you, please." After a second, though, I heard the nurse exhale with relief.

"Got it. Whew." It was not his first rodeo. We didn't know it yet, but it wouldn't be our last.

If this had been all the drama we absorbed that year, I would hesitate to use the word *trauma* to describe it. An unexpected surgery is not in and of itself always trauma. But this one came after the sale of our house in Ohio fell through, leaving us paying two mortgages plus West Coast rent. This surgery came in the midst of an extended harassment situation at my new job that necessitated a level of outside consultation and legal research not unheard of in ministry, but still pretty rare. Financial strain had started interfering with my ability to breathe, and now the surgery also meant we would have only my income for a while. All of it weighed invisibly on me as I settled into the waiting room only to be called up to the desk far too soon.

"The surgeon would like to meet with you across the hall."

An update, I assumed. They had told me to expect four to six hours of waiting, depending on how much ductwork needed to be reconstructed.

"What's wrong?" I asked the surgeon.

"Has Adam had any cardiac issues before?"

"He's never even sick," I said.

"Well, his heart stopped."

We had not noticed. We had not noticed the ways his body slowed down when mine sped up or the greenish tinge that had crept into his skin over the last year. We had not noticed so many things.

In the Temple

after five a hospital quiets
turning inward
floor by floor
wing by wing
to the hard slow work of healing
call buttons beep
door latches smack
but the business of medicine hushes itself
to trust
(there is nothing left to do)
in the Body
to wait
on its powers
with more or less
patience prayer medicine

Priests at Work

Something about a hospital unnerves.

Perhaps especially a hospital as large as this tower on the hill. Here, the body's frailties and limitations are every day in full view, not hidden away where we prefer to keep them, but in your face.

A man of broad, strong, military bearing faces me as the elevator door opens, one arm ending in a stump above the elbow. I cannot exit to my floor without looking at him. All of him. Later, in the quiet after hours, the doors open and I enter the elevator automatically, surprised by a tiny older woman with tubes running from her nose, rolling an oxygen tank. A seven-year-old girl with cascading brown curls and blue eyes stares with a gaze that strikes me as neither scared nor blasé but simply set behind her yellow face mask as blue-shirted transport staff roll her down the hallway. A shrunken, yellowed possessor of a new-to-him kidney with almost no hair pushes his IV pole ambitiously through the crowd, floating not unlike a mildly angry angel in his hospital gown. Among the suits and the ties, the white coats and the blue scrubs, the bald, naked body exposes its wounds and scars.

I've spent nearly a week here, and I still can't keep myself from flinching. Does one get used to this? It is so unlike the outside world with its power walking and power lunching, cross-fitting and feeling the burn, thirty-day cleanses supplemented with essential oils for young living. Out there, perishables negotiate for longevity, bartering and begging and believing they can live longer, live stronger.

In here, each day, all day, in the surgical waiting room, parents and children and spouses and lovers and friends watch randomly assigned numbers change on a large blue screen, signaling in coded colors the relative vulnerability of their loved ones' bodies: Pre-op. Operating. Closing. Recovery.

People here wait to spy the color change that will permit them to breathe, finally, over their puzzles or knitting or laptops that have

occupied only half of their mind while the other half has been hop-
ing simply, "Please let it work. Please live."

Two weeks after the "heart event" that halted the first surgery
attempt, we are back at the big research hospital on the hill, this
time armed with the knowledge that my husband's heart, when
stressed, sometimes opts to just stop. That's what had happened two
weeks earlier when his abdomen got pumped full of gas for the "min-
imally invasive" operation that is most common.

A cardiovascular pause.

Whereas most of our heart rates speed up under stress or intense
pain, in patients like him the heart rate and blood pressure can suddenly drop. It's called vasovagal reflex or neurocardiogenic syncope.
The cyst still needed to come out, but this time the surgeons were
doing it old school cutting an incision halfway across the abdomen,
with a central line inserted down his jugular so they could manually
restart his heart "just in case."

I tried to distract myself as I ate breakfast alone in the cafeteria,
fluids dripping from my eyes and nose as I looked out the window
toward the clouded-over river valley. Then I moved upstairs, tried to
knit, attempted to hack away at a newsletter article that was over-
due, gave up, and went to the lobby to watch people instead.

Nearing forty years of age myself, I was disquieted by the un-
abashed brokenness of bodies, their displayed disease.

Do the physicians and surgeons and nurses see instead the body's
power to heal? Do they staple, suture, and insert IVs with confidence
and awe at what the body can bear and survive? Are the priests of
this temple startled into an opposite response . . . worship?

The gas fireplace in the lobby, ten feet long and pebbled with
singed glass beads the color of earth and sea, could be stared into
from both sides.

There was a time when priests were doctors not of divinity alone
but also of the human body. For centuries, religious professionals
offered healing services for body, mind, and spirit. Monks grew herbs
and crafted remedies. Nuns changed linens and made poultices for
the sick. In 1747, the father of Methodism published his own little book of medical wisdom, mostly a compilation of advice from

surgeons, physicians, and apothecaries whose works he had studied and repackaged alphabetically together with his own—simple and affordable—in keeping with his concern for the overlooked poor.

"Real" doctors of the time criticized John Wesley for trying to make a buck off of quack remedies, though most of the field was hardly more medically advanced. Wesley retorted that far too many physicians of the era handpicked their patients from the wealthy classes or prolonged treatment plans for their own financial gain. *Primitive Physick; or an Easy and Natural Method of Curing Most Diseases* (London: Thomas Tyre, 1747) ended up becoming one of the most popular booklets published in eighteenth-century England and was repeatedly reprinted in Philadelphia between 1764 and 1791.[1]

I'm grateful for the advances of science and medicine, that I have Lexapro to support my body in managing the anxiety brought on by childhood trauma rather than a daily regimen of head scrubbing with vinegar, as Wesley advised. I do wonder whether we've lost some of those priestly physician priorities in caring for the health of the poor.

While I was in and out of the hospital waiting for Adam to be discharged, I received news that a young man in one of my former youth groups had died by suicide. Across the miles and years, I could do nothing but send fruit. I was no longer his soul's doctor, and there was no way to know if any remedy of mine would have made a difference anyway.

Once the soft ovoid tissue density had been removed, my lover's abdomen sported a seven-inch scar, its purple puckers held together with some magical skin glue, on the topmost layer of several stitched back together after being sliced through on purpose: a hurt meant to heal.

Not all hurts do.

---

1. Samuel J. Rogal, "Pills for the Poor: John Wesley's *Primitive Physick*," *The Yale Journal of Biology and Medicine* 51, no. 1 (1978): 81–90.

The Body Remembers

Nine months postsurgery, we hike for our Friday night date night, thankful the light is long when our budget is tight. He has just run a half marathon. Most of the time, he says, the surgery that gave him the scar, so far receded now, feels like a story that happened to someone else.

But not always.

Sometimes dimmed memory surfaces viscerally. For a moment the light will shimmer the way it did under the influence of pain-killers in that recovery room. Or he will feel a twinge deep in his abdomen where, one organ missing, the cells still occasionally bump into detours as they knit sinew to sinew, connect tissue, move fluid.

"My body now has a map of pain it didn't have before," Adam says.

Involuntarily, my steps halt. I inhale a protective cushion of air around the small black hole his words poke open inside me.

"Mm, hmm," I murmur, and try again to breathe.

The body remembers.

Somewhere in the middle of The Really Hard Years, I sat in a pool of lamplight late at night, straining my eyes past midnight over two bamboo needles in the corner of the living room. Passing a creamy cotton over my left index finger, I was trying to finish a stuffed tooth fairy pillow before the small tooth wobbling in my kindergartner's gumline popped out on its own. I was running out of time.

With all quiet in the creaking, near-century-old home, I worked accompanied only by the occasional tap of the bamboo making loops and the whisper of soft cotton slipping from needle to needle.

Suddenly, she was there. Unbidden, unthought, and all around me.

I inhaled sharply. Stopped knitting. Tears came.

You may think I'm crazy, but I'll risk it.

I don't believe in ghosts or occult mysteries, and yet I will tell you that I felt the presence of my friend Kristi in that moment all around me. Kristi, who hosted the Kentucky Derby party to which I hauled my still bruised and bleeding body scarcely eight days postpartum, desperate to leave the house and beaming in that terrified new-parent way over the small reddish creature entrusted to my care. Kristi, who gave me a box of hand-knit baby beanies made to look like fruit and veggie tops. Kristi, whose "throw-anywhere" scrap picnic quilt my family used and uses still almost weekly. Kristi, who kept us all rolling with laughter and tears at the knit night at the pub where she'd invited me, to make desperately needed friends, the two of us sharing an isolating career.

Kristi, who died at thirty-eight from a galloping colon cancer that refused to let her celebrate even her first wedding anniversary.

I did not check the calendar until the next day, when I saw the buttons knit with "K" we wore to her memorial appear in just a few places on social media.

My body remembered the day she died before my mind did.

More recently, my body remembered on the physical therapist's table.

During the nonchalant business of discussing the arrangements for her vacation replacement the following week, I realized my physical therapist's recommended sub was male.

"Will he . . . will he be doing what you've been doing?" I asked, with half my buttocks exposed so she could apply a pain patch to the piriformis doing so much mischief to my SI joint and sciatic nerve.

She asked if I was comfortable with a male therapist, and I stuttered a bit.

"I . . . I don't usually."

She didn't miss a beat.

"Have you had sexual trauma?" she asked. "Many of my patients have." Par for the course, evidently, for medical professionals specializing in pelvis, hip, and pelvic floor health.

"Huh . . . well, how do I put this?" I externalized my processing, face down still in the sticky vinyl cradle. "Let's just say it was corporal punishment taken too far."

"You were beaten, then?"

Her bluntness took me aback. I was still prone, staring at the floor.

"I only got welts once that I remember," I said. "My brother got it worse, I think. On the scale of terrible things that can happen to a kid, I guess . . . I guess it could have been worse."

That line about my brother getting it worse was a story I had told myself for years. I had repeated it out loud only recently to the small number of people to whom the words had tumbled out: my spouse, that physical therapist, a friend. I had assumed, maybe even wanted to believe, that as the boy two years younger and the child forever getting into scrapes, my father hadn't withheld his punishing anger from his son. It was my brother who nearly drove the Nova down the hill into the highway at an age so young his feet barely dangled off the driver's side of the bench seat behind the wheel. It was my brother who drilled holes in the arms of the living room furniture, the one who tried to fix a broken light fixture in the basement with a screwdriver on his own. He'd gotten mildly electrocuted and knocked out before any of us knew why the lights had flickered on the floors above. It was my brother who seemed to stumble headlong into transgression—sledding onto the neighbor's roof—seemingly unable to help himself. I'd been the cautious one, reading each scene to calculate the danger. When he slipped the gears of the Nova into neutral that day we played in the driveway at the top of the hill, I was there in the back seat, helpfully offering my two-years-older wisdom, "I don't think that's a good . . . turn the wheel! Turn the wheel! Turn the wheel!"

It's not that I wanted my little brother to have suffered more trauma, but surely my God-fearing father wouldn't have hit his little girl, already too old for spankings, harder than he'd hit his boy. Or, at least, surely we had gotten the same?

I had never checked with my brother though.

At the next family get-together, the two of us went for a run. Getting out of the small house full of babies and toddlers and school-aged cousins yelling and throwing wasn't the only reason I managed to actually get out of bed and dressed by 6:15 a.m. as planned.

"I have a question for you," I said, panting between phrases. "You don't have to answer, if you don't want to." I told the revisited memory, welts and all, while trying to jog four miles alongside him on a wooded trail. "I realized on that physical therapist's bench, it isn't about sexuality or attraction. I feel vulnerable and unsafe in a space where a man has power over my body. And there's a good reason."

"Do you have any memories like that?" I asked him. "Did you get it worse?"

"I remember the torture of being sent out to pick my own switch," he said with that wry half-laugh we used to soften the edge of hard family stories. Then, after a pause, "I don't remember getting any welts."

I tried once, as a gesture against gender discrimination, to just go with it when my usual massage therapist canceled sick and her backup was male. It was the most uncomfortable, awkward massage I've ever endured. And the part I may most regret is that I only had one bill in cash in my purse. I ended up leaving a tip much more generous than I could afford for a massage therapist I never wanted to see again. I hadn't understood why then.

Within the span of just a few years missing pieces can fall into place in a way that finally makes some sense of the story one person's skin has been holding within.[1] I could try to tally all the potential factors: the harassers who followed me across the street, that one night at kickboxing practice, a poverty simulation sponsored by local non-profits where I completely lost my cool, filling out a training worksheet about adverse childhood experiences on another day only to see my early life staring back at me. And, of course, that one day at physical therapy.

Who knows how or why or when one particular body decides to tell its truth?

The body remembers. It always remembers.

---

1. Bessel Van Der Kolk, *The Body Keeps the Score: Brain, Mind, and Body in the Healing of Trauma* (New York: Penguin Books, 2014), the most comprehensive and accessible scientific research on the human body and trauma.

Tremor

I.

From which tree did this pear fall? My father's father was a cypher, a silent maker creator painter who attended three art schools before enlisting to clerk for an officer following the Western front East in a car my grandfather hand-lettered and logoed with a grinning cartoon before framing the liberated dead and emaciated living in photographs he never sent home or wanted to talk about for all the years he returned weekends and not every one from color correcting printer films at that Toledo factory.

He bent alone over wood and metal projects in a basement lined with canned fruits while his sons fought over cars with silence guns and blows.

II.

What do I do now with this quivering lip, creeping tremble of age involuntarily breaking beneath your grayed and age-pocked face? This tremble now in your hands coring an apple yanks my heart toward compassion, an involuntary muscle movement that remembers my own legs quaking in a pine tree skirted hideaway or cowered beneath a gnarled table in the living room driven there by rage exploding, silencing our pealing laughter unaware of your mid-day slumber.

I look away from your fragility try to quiet my shakes by force of sheer grown will.

III.

"You were beaten, then?" Nothing like rape or incest, I assure, these revelations of sexual trauma commonplace, I learn, on the physical therapist's bench. "I only got welts once that I remember," I say. "My brother got it worse." As if there is a worse or better thirty years later when a grown woman getting a little PT for a running injury suddenly can feel the raised and red stripes left raw and hot by leather across the skin of buttocks and thighs long-since healed.

As if even now she fears hearing, "Stop crying, or I'll give you something to really cry about."

IV.

My lover's voice is muffled. "You don't have to be quiet. The kids aren't home." And I laugh the way a ripe pear bursts at a bite, juice running down my skin, a pear so ripe and full it can no longer be hidden in a crumpled paper bag carried somewhere else I can only let the juice drip down the side of my palm across my wrist where his lips try to intercept but miss as the nectar slides to my elbow and I laugh because this cannot be taken from me.

Falling back, I laugh and I laugh at the hidden waves rippling, a tremor carrying me over the edge into that nameless freely being, into our recovered garden.

V: DEATH

Celebration of Life

The smell of cat excrement didn't hit me until I had pushed aside a gift bag to sit down on the loveseat, the only clear surface in sight. Eyes watering, nostrils burning, I look to the floor and nearby surfaces, scanning for the source. Beneath my book bag? I hope it's not on my purse. I try to brush the cushion nonchalantly before taking my seat, to move the cat hair a bit. It was stained, I judged, but it was not fresh. Please let me not be wrong. With the side of my shoe, I nudge a grimy box of VHS tapes a little to the left to expose more of the matted carpet. On second thought, no; better not to look.

It's hard not to smell when I breathe, though I try to do so for the ninety minutes we sit to plan the memorial service. He makes tea, which I'm glad to have warming my hand. I drink it until the black Siamese named Tony Stark pushes his face into my mug. I recall some hazy statistic about Siamese being among the breeds most prone to worms and intestinal disease. I do not touch my drink again.

The living room floor shows only glimpses of mottled blue carpet turned litter box, piled with magazines, books, boxes, and more cat hair. A basket of balled yarn sits by the recliner in the corner, an unfinished crochet project on top, pea-colored feline diarrhea dried in a puddle across the lacework in progress and the top-most ball of aqua blue yarn.

I stifle the urge to scream and run, imagining fleas and roaches hiding, praying there are none even as we talk.

They don't know exactly how he died.

Keeping the house at forty degrees in January helped preserve the body, they think, though preserved is not the word I'd use to describe what his verbally abused ex-partner of thirty years found on that queen-sized mattress, now propped sideways against a column on the patio to air out, to dry.

I can't see the bloody side from here.

I'm grateful for that.

Murmuring over photos as I tuck them into my file, the dis-jointed stories fall out: The time he pushed him down. The time he sold his husband's new bike while he was away at work. The names he called him. The one time he wrapped a handmade wooden doll-house and Christmas presents for a family down on their luck.

Mean. Abusive. Alcoholic. Ill.

And still, he asks, "Can we call it a 'Celebration of Life'?"

My God.

Even one this mean, stained with cat crap and bruises and blood?

Yes.

Yes, we will.

Read This Sign

No woman wailed over Dennis's body. He died the way so many people fear: alone. For several days they did not discover him on the couch in the subsidized apartment he was so proud to have finally earned. Officially, he died of "natural causes." Regularly soak your internal organs in alcohol for forty years, and your liver will quite naturally quit, too.

We all knew he'd fallen off the wagon. He'd lost his keys. The trustees hesitated to issue him new ones, and he'd borne his complaint to me in soured skin and yellowed eyes. I accomplished the unenviable task of reminding him that if he showed up on church property or to his work shift drunk, he'd have to go home. The last time I spoke with him, he drunk-dialed. We all tried to offer help. For a few days, our cell phone messages met only silence. Truthfully, he had often disappeared for two weeks at a time only to show up again, penitent, for his shift. This time, he did not.

The local funeral director was no booster of the food pantry where Dennis worked—and especially of the way pantry customers crowded the church's fine atrium during morning funerals. I would have been pleased if he'd shown basic respect toward Dennis. I was surprised by his kindness and tact. He was tender. He spoke no ill of the dead. He waited patiently as the estranged family hesitated far too long at the graveside, waiting. Waiting for what?

Dennis left his mark around that church in many ways. But the most obvious signs of Dennis's presence were his signs. Many, many signs. The signs Dennis posted around the building featured not just a single symbol or a key word or two, but often entire epistles, complete messages carefully crammed onto an eight-by-ten-inch sheet of paper. Even several years after his death, the food pantry walls were still papered with Dennis's signs filled with detailed instructions for this or that food pantry protocol. Just in case you missed his first-tier signs, he made additional signs pointing with big black arrows, reiterating: "Read this sign!"

Occasionally, Dennis's signage overflowed onto the front door of our atrium so much that passersby could no longer see through the glass.

I miss Dennis. And his signs.

Compassionate and hardworking, Dennis gave generously even when he did not have much himself. Small, thoughtful gifts or cards from the dollar store. He cared deeply about helping those in need, until he sensed someone was scamming the system. Then he raged. His temper flared. And there were certain demons that Dennis fought his whole life long.

Dennis loved gardens and being outside. A year before his death, he carefully planted bright red geraniums, among other things, in the flower bed between the church's entrance on the downtown square and the courthouse next door. Right behind the geraniums sprouted one of Dennis's signs: "Thou Shalt Not Litter—Enjoy the Flowers!" We sang "In the Garden" at his funeral because I imagined Dennis would love to be there, with Mary Magdalene, meeting the Risen Christ.

Every human life speaks. Each person is a whole book. And the book of Dennis's life—a self-bound bundle of a lifetime of home-made signs—told a rough and stained story of grace. In his struggle to keep giving, even when he felt others abused his or God's generosity. In his struggles to fight the demons of alcoholism and mental illness. Living with Dennis forced our church staff to constantly revisit questions about that mystery we Christians call grace, and what it means to be people who live out that grace.

Jesus gets called the Word. He shows up as a sign made of skin and bones. In Dennis's life, God carefully wrote again the same message God gave us in Jesus. Only this time, God crammed that message into the form of one complicated but incredibly compassionate person and surrounded it with giant arrows: "Read this sign!"

I used the honorarium from Dennis's service to buy flowers that year: perennials and impatiens for the front beds, a pair of blueberry bushes for the backyard. The blueberry bushes did not survive. I'd planted them too close to the place heavy rains pooled in the middle of the yard, and the following spring brought record rainfall. The greenhouse man told me, "They don't like to have their feet wet." The card in the pot warned me, too, to place in well-drained soil.

I did not read the sign.

Seeing Death

"Remember how short our life is,
How frail indeed You have made us.
Who can live and not see death?"

—*Psalm 89:47–48*[1]

Who can live and not see death? A lot of Americans, apparently. Or, so they believe.

What the songwriter takes as a given simply is not for many people in the United States today. We don't see death if we can help it. If we do, we don't talk about it. Where would we in a culture where the dead get whisked behind heavy curtains, made up with blush and perfumed with flowers before judged presentable enough to "view"?

I posed the question to my online social network: Have you seen a dead body outside of a funeral home?

Stories tumbled out of sitting with departed parents, of family members who waited for vigil keepers to step out of hospital rooms before breathing their last, of career-altering encounters in the ER, of unsettling death rattles and the efficient tenderness of a nurse who slipped off a man's wedding band and put it in a freshly widowed hand without saying a word.

Have you seen a dead body outside of a funeral home? I have. And once, a whole room full. I am not entirely sure it was legal, so in order to protect the innocent, I will say that once a medical school student from my college dorm offered a private tour of their cadaver lab, which I accepted without waiting a beat.

After hours, the lab was quiet and bright, even without over-head lights. I did not touch a thing. My tour guide was excited,

---

1. Robert Benson, "Day 17 Psalter: Evening," Psalm 89, *Venite: A Book of Daily Prayer* (Nashville: Abingdon Press, 2017), 161.

though, thrilled to show his growing expertise and awe of the human body.

The cadavers all knowingly donated their bodies for research. The student teams did not get to pick. Bodies were assigned. And they often surprised. One that appeared large and thick could be an athlete with little fatty tissue to obscure tendons, nerves, muscle, and bone. Easier to dissect. Another might look small but be filled with fat cells and disease—like smoker's lungs—frustrating students tasked with identifying the various organs' healthy parts.

We spoke in hushed tones as my tour guide folded back the draping on his team's human: a woman. They had recently excavated and studied her uterus, her womb.

"Are there rules," I asked, "for how you treat them? I mean, like, how to be respectful?"

I guess I was trying to imagine my dead body being handled by twenty-five-year-old hands, my organs, the knees my lover cupped, or the womb that swelled with blood and squeezed it out so rhythmically each month for years, that uterus that twice now has muscled a fresh human into the air or water of this world.

"Oh, yes," the nearly doctor said. As students, they were so grateful for the gift of actual human bodies, their variation, their magnificence. "A lot of med schools even do a ritual of sorts, a dedication before dissection starts."

Some, like Stanford's School of Medicine, begin with a moment of silence before the bags around the donated bodies are unzipped. Others recite prayers and bow their heads while a priest offers a blessing over the shrouds. Campbell University's School of Osteopathy holds a white rose ceremony in which each medical student brings a white rose from their table to place in a vase that gets delivered to the not-yet-dead while the chaplain or a professor offers a nondenominational and extemporaneous prayer. Oregon Health and Sciences University holds a memorial service for the families of the cadavers they respectfully refer to as their "first patient."

A medical student from Yale recites a version of Psalm 139. Another, at Ohio State University's College of Medicine, quotes C. S. Lewis on self-giving.

At Loyola University of Chicago's Stritch School of Medicine, faculty and chaplains and students take turns remembering the fullness of the cadavers' lives as well as the humility and humanity of those who will learn from them. A Jesuit priest who is also a physician often reminds the students that they may learn something about the person's life that even the person themself did not know while they loved and ached on this planet. Evergreen branches from campus are dipped in holy water, which students then sprinkle at each bay holding a body while another student slowly reads,

Creator God, we are mindful that these bodies before us have already been blessed by you. Throughout their lives, they embodied your blessing through their presence, work, and relationships. We pause to be grateful for the hidden gifts of blessing which they will be for us in the coming weeks. Bless them, bless those who loved them and knew them, and bless us as we learn from them. Amen.[2]

The students then hang the evergreen sprigs in the lab as a reminder of this blessing throughout the course. At the close of the course, students once again look to the evergreen branches pinned to the bulletin board to reflect and share all that they have learned about medicine and about themselves.

So important was this ritual to Loyola medical students, they asked to do it even during the pandemic of 2020, joining over video conference software, while two staff members in PPE performed the ritual in the lab.[3]

The teachers of gross anatomy know how much one dead body can teach.

"The cadaver keeps speaking to you even in death," said Michael Dauzvardis, then-director of the anatomy course at Loyola back in 2011. "You've got to listen to it. There are volumes of knowledge you can still learn from that person who made the ultimate gift."[4]

---

2. Author's notes from interview with and material provided by Julie DeMareo, Health Sciences Campus Ministry chaplain at Loyola University of Chicago, June 10, 2021.

3. Author's notes, interview with Julie DeMareo.

4. McClatchy-Tribune News Service, "The Profane and the Sacred: Blessing Ceremony at Catholic University's Cadaver Lab Acknowledges the Balance," September 15, 2011, *https://www. reporterherald.com/2011/09/15/the-profane-and-the-sacred-blessing-ceremony-at-catholic-universitys-cadaver-lab-acknowledges-the-balance/*.

Tissue procurement organizations speak of the same generosity and awe. When a soldier shot in Afghanistan regains the use of his arm, or a woman who had polio as a child finds relief after more than fifty surgeries on her legs failed to eliminate her pain, or someone on the list gets a lifesaving valve or kidney, the wonder of the body can overshadow even death.

"I always enjoyed watching the healing process of the body," says a friend of mine who works in organ and tissue donation. "To watch what we can do with medicine, how certain things can be restored or saved. I get to see a lot more of the hopeful side of it and the impact on the recipient. That sure keeps me going."

"When I would see the patient, the state of death is so ugly," my friend says. "But the first time I did a baby, I didn't see the ugliness of death. It was beautiful."

This Door

This door looks no different than the others in its row
this one, with the holiday flag still stuck in the flower bed
this door seals inside the nervous anxiety of people gathered around
the one thing making the room strange
a corpse
from which all of us, with varying success, avert our eyes
laughing, crying,
sitting in awkward silence, waiting
while the Corgi pees again at the foot of the bed
"How far *does* that VNA nurse have to drive?"
a sentence or two from the 21st chapter of Revelation
and *His Eye Is On the Sparrow*
(just the refrain)
a cell phone rings out Beethoven's *Ode to Joy*
we exhale our ode to death
and wait
for some return to life

Lazarus Comes Home from Chicago

For a season, death and I seemed to show up at all the same parties. The two of us becoming familiar friends. I started counting after forty-five months as pastor of a congregation, when I had already personally officiated forty-two funerals and memorial services. Pulpit pinch-hitters fielded a handful more while I was out for a brief maternity leave. In total, I buried sixty-eight people in five and a half years before I left that church.

Being death's warm-up act and closer can make you a lousy guest at a cocktail party. Imagine this exchange at the bar: "How was work today?" "Oh, well, you know, 'ashes to ashes' and a ride in a hearse." Living with death does not make for great small talk. But it can give you a peculiar vision. You regularly gaze through a doorway other people keep tightly shut.

We live in one of the most death-averse societies on the planet. We go to great lengths to avoid even saying the word *death*, using instead a plethora of euphemisms: passed away, passed on, passed into glory, went home. But we deny death in other ways, too. A parishioner of mine who worked at a nursing home told me once that as staff they were not allowed to tell residents when another resident had died. Of course, when Betty across the hall notices that Gwen's room is suddenly empty, swept clean, and the bed made, if she has any presence of mind, she's going to ask the next nurse where Gwen went. The nurse is instructed to use code known only to the staff: "Oh, Gwen moved to Chicago." This usually satisfies, my informant admitted. But once, when a resident asked a nurse where dear old Bob with the oxygen mask had disappeared to, she spoke tenderly, compassionately.

"I'm sorry," she said. "But he's gone to Chicago."

At which point the resident, not understanding the code phrase, opined, "I don't know . . . Chicago's not really that bad."

Even nurses who help people die must avoid speaking that one ultimate reality we try hard to forget: death is always at the door. Some of us know we stand closer to that threshold than others even though all of us are only ever seconds away.

Mary and Martha and Jesus did not have the luxury of denial. Like so many people in so many cultures—up until quite recently, really—for these three, death was a regular household guest. Everyone entered the world at home. And everyone left the world at home. Both were equally messy and painful and precarious events.

In "Crapper,"[1] Thomas Lynch tells one of my favorite stories about a woman whose wake became notorious because, surprised by a heart attack, she had not enough advanced notice to switch to bland foods or even consume nothing at all as her time on earth neared its expiration. She had instead the night before eaten and drunk great quantities of her favorites—rich and gassy. Which made the room where her body was laid out and the party over it a most memorable olfactory experience, foreshortened by the intense smell of gastrointestinal distress.

For all its high theology and abstract signs and metaphors, John's version of the Jesus story at least pulls no punches on the gritty details of human cells decomposing, that a friend dead three days "stinketh." That famous line happened when these three friends—Jesus, Mary, and Martha—made a brief visit to Chicago together. Jesus has been trying to keep an arm's length from Jerusalem, where the powers that be were increasingly hostile toward him. But while he was away, he got word that his good friend Lazarus was sick. Then Lazarus died. Jesus used a euphemism that his disciples at first did not understand: "Our friend Lazarus has fallen asleep."[2]

Jesus and the disciples risked their own deaths to go pay their respects, and Lazarus's two sisters came out to meet them. Once again in John, two women get right to the heart of the theological issue: Where were you, God?

---

1. Thomas Lynch, "Crapper," in *The Undertaking: Life Studies from the Dismal Trade* (New York: W. W. Norton, 1997), 39.

2. John 11:11.

"If you had been here, my brother would not have died," Martha said. "But even now I know that God will give you whatever you ask."[3]

Jesus offered her what sounded at first like typical religious consolation: "Your brother will rise again."

Martha knew those old hymns: "When the Role Is Called Up Yonder," "O, When the Saints Go Marching In." She had been raised to find consolation in God's *future* promises of "the sweet by and by."

She said, "I know he will rise again on the last day." That's when Jesus said, in effect, the salvation I bring is bigger than that. The Good News I proclaim is bigger than that.

"I AM the resurrection *and* the life."[4] Eternal life is God's gift to you not just on the last day, but today and tomorrow and every day. Then he called Lazarus back to life to show just how permeable the wall really is between the world we can see and know and the life that is beyond.

Lazarus came home from Chicago.

This sign so upsets the powers that be that Lazarus got put on a hit list. Some of the movers and shakers vowed not only to kill Jesus but to get rid of Lazarus, too. Eternal life threatened death's power. Jesus led Martha and Mary to the doorway, and they got a glimpse through.

I really want to know how it smelled.

When death shows up on our doorsteps we tend to be more receptive to the vision Jesus gave Mary and Martha than on other days. For this reason, perhaps, I end many funerals with some version of the blessing of Swiss mystic and philosopher Henri Frédéric Amiel: "Life is short. We do not have too much time to gladden the hearts of those who travel the way with us. So, be swift to love. And make haste to be kind." The blessing reminds those gathered that Christ's resurrection never was, nor will be, just for "the last day." It is for today, and tomorrow, and every day we walk through the valley of the shadow of death. You don't have to wait until you are dead

---

3. John 11:21.
4. John 11:25.

and gone to live with God, to be in "that better place." Life is short. Be in that better place now. I AM the resurrection and the life, Jesus said. I am the life *after* death, and I am the life *before* death. I AM both. I AM here. And I AM after.

If Jesus is to be believed, Chicago isn't so bad. At least, it's not a place to be feared, though the drive or flight there might be painful and stink dreadfully.

As I flipped through my funeral files that one week, adding up the first forty-two lives mainly out of curiosity, I pictured them together as a congregation, living and moving in God's presence— Carol and Dick (aged and kind), Tom and Tom (both middle-aged), Brittany and David (barely out of childhood)—all of them moving, laughing, living with God. It is a Christian conviction that we can see those people through the door made by Christ. We are not as far-removed from them as we sometimes feel. We continue to live with them here *and* after. By suffering, dying, and rising, Christ shows us, as he showed Mary and Martha in John, the veil between the temporal and the eternal is much thinner than we'd like to admit. Through his death, Jesus flung open a doorway between the "here" and the "after." In a way, he became the doorway.

I can feel myself stepping through it on All Saints Days when I bring the baseball, the book, the ball of yarn, the rubber factory worker ID badge, into a sanctuary of lighted candles. Every annual journey through Holy Week brings us near that threshold. And every celebration of the Eucharist, too, as I stand with broken bread in my hands in a place where past, present, and future meet in a body, a whole cosmos contained within skin.

This door. This door was made for us.

VI: WATER

Reborn through Water

My mother prayed for me; she was worried when the window of her hopefulness following my older sister's birth lengthened longer than a year, then two. I finally arrived after three, in mid-November, a product of the "Blizzard of '78" that earlier in the year had socked Northeast Ohio in white and gray drifts for weeks.

Radical Jesus hippies, they planned to welcome me at home, not in the hospital where she had barely arrived in time to deliver her first. So, the waters of my embryonic home broke in my first home built of wood. My father, sporting swim trunks in photos documenting the aftermath, had run to fill up the cramped blue porcelain bathtub to ease labor, just in case.

Snow and water. My conception and my birth. Water courses through wildernesses in my life like arteries and veins in the earth, washing, running, pouring over rocks, cutting the hardest stone.

I cannot remember my own baptism, though I am told it occurred days after my birth. Less than a week, in fact. I imagine it happened in a living room, perhaps with Tom or one of those other Brethren-rebel-Orthodox seminarians and single-so-far men of our house church circled 'round. I'm certain there were bell-bottoms and wide-collared men's dress shirts. The next baptism I remember was a cousin's, water poured in a proper font in the otherwise dry Methodist church planted at a crossroads between cornfields in the flat western half of the state. My father was asked to stand as godfather, the only other openly religious sibling my uncle could tap. After that? I don't remember my own siblings' baptisms; except for those two Methodists, none of my other cousins went to church.

Rushing around before the service in my first church, officiating my very first baptism, I asked the deacons for a pitcher and got blank stares in return. "I want to pour the water," I explained, "not just leave it still in the bowl." We found something made of clear plastic, an adequate stand-in for crystal, but I vowed to hunt through all the curio and antique shops on my days off and vacation until I could find a vessel worthy of showing off the waters of new life.

When I left that job on schedule at the end of two years, that same deacon gave me a large ceramic pitcher, thrown by an artist, swirling with glazes of blue and brown, both water and the dirt from which we are made. I use it still a decade later to pour either water or wine.

It was through my child, born under a water sign and born literally into water, that I was reminded of the power of rebirth. Eight whole years after I drew him out of the water, to the surface of that birthing tub, we were snuggled on a couch reading one of his favorite fantasy authors, the tale of an ancient family of Egyptian magicians by the name of Kane. Remember the law of conservation, a parent warns the young hero in The Red Pyramid: "Energy and matter can't be created or destroyed, only changed."[1]

"Sometimes changed for the better."

Energy and matter can't be destroyed. Only changed.

That's what the water does. Change energy and matter, so that unlike Lazarus, who came back to this life in the same old body, we may say together, "I believe in the resurrection of the body and the life everlasting."

---

1. Rick Riordan, The Red Pyramid (New York: Hyperion Books, 2010), 502–3.

Seventy-Eight Percent:
A Bio-Graphy[1]

Forgetting for a moment how exactly I wrapped the bath sheet around my trunk and simultaneously disrobed, I know the terry cloth has passed around my shoulders one too many times. Did the towel go under first? I can't remember. But I'm grateful no one is nearby as I flash one hip, one butt cheek, then the opposite breast.

The steam room at this spa is my favorite. But it's been a while.

Turning toward the little table where there usually sits a bowl of wrapped washcloths submerged in ice water like wine coolers and served with tongs next to a plate of orange wedges for refreshment post-steam, I'm disappointed. Only the spray bottle of eucalyptus oil is there now. Maybe they'll replenish the treats by the time I'm out.

I pull open the door and in the midst of the vacuum sucking sound see another person through the steam, naked on a towel.

She starts. "Oh. Time to wrap up," pulling the corners of the towel up from the bench on either side.

"I don't mind either way," I say, crossing in front of her, with my eyes staring ahead. "However you're comfortable is fine with me."

She relaxes, then lets the towel fall back to her sides.

"Dis is such a grreat steam room," she says. "I wouldn't do it if it was both. But since it's just vwimen . . . Dis is more comfortable." She pronounces every syllable separately. "I'm European," she continues. "Men, vwimen together, we don't cover up. I feel silly vith my cloths."

Her explanation reminds me of the day my teenage self was plunged wide-eyed into another cultural view of the human body at

---

1. "78% H2O" is an Ani DiFranco song on the album *Reprieve*, Righteous Babe Music / BMI, 2006, and definitely an influence on this meditation.

a Japanese spa, a day-off excursion that I'm sure our hosts intended to be a treat for the evangelical tour group in which I sang and mimed. No, I'm not proud of it. I did enjoy the trip, notwithstanding the awkward moments seared into my brain when conservative teenagers and twentysomethings froze at being invited to strip down before entering the coed baths.

"Have you ever been to Japan?" I ask. "They have wonderful spas and hot springs, and it is the same there as you. Women's area. Men's area. And the most traditional a mix of both, coed, no one covers. It's just bodies, all kinds, no big deal."

"Yes, yes," she says. "I have heard dat, too."

"I'm afraid we Americans are a little uptight," I offer apologetically. And though I say this, I tug upward on the towel slipping too low across my breast, daring to expose a nipple, and watch sweat beads form on my left shoulder.

I wonder again why we are so embarrassed by the naked body, as I inhale deep, moist steam.

In my new home, I save up to buy these fifteen minutes of luxurious humidity, to feel the steam bathe and cleanse my face, my lungs. It comes free with the massage here, and if I'm not running too late, I duck in both before and after. Then I wash away the oil and sweat with luxury organic soaps stocked in the locker room, feeling just a little guilty for the expense of the soaps and the amount of hot water used. I do conserve the towels, in an attempt to balance it all out, using just one from steam room through towel dry.

This is so different from the place where I was born near the great inland sea of the Great Lakes, where in my youth the water seemed abundant and eternal, a nuisance even when late-July thunderstorms brought flash floods to the bottom of our hill near a manufactured reservoir or the rain pelted the canvas sides of our tent camper for the better part of a week's camping vacation. Moisture-saturated air oppressed us most of the summer, and I'm sure the little house church thought nothing of how much water they used when I was baptized one November mere days after my birth.

In Ohio, where we had no air conditioning, on summer nights it wasn't the heat that drove us mad but the humidity, when the temperature barely nudged a few degrees lower after nightfall and we lay in the least amount of clothes possible on top of sweat-soaked sheets. In 100 percent humidity, just ninety-five degrees Fahrenheit can feel like the bowels of hell itself. Water was abundant there, so much so I took it for granted. Our well was always full. The only time we went without enough to wash or bathe was when the machines broke or the tile in the run-down bathroom crumbled on our heads.

My biogeography now straddles two differing ecosystems. I write these words partway through November, from a cabin high in the Fremont-Winema National Forest in the Cascade Range, where typically by now a foot of snow is already settled on the ground. Not this year. This year there is still a sign in the fire pit prohibiting fires due to the wildfire risk. We've seen only one and a half inches of precipitation since May. I'm at 5,600 feet elevation or so, which receives about fifty-four inches of snowfall each year. By my birthday later this month there should already be snow in the upper elevations, but for the third year in a row we are in drought. The frozen crust of earth is still bare, and I wonder about the health and future of Crater Lake, not far from here, an ancient volcanic pool filled with the clearest water on the planet because it is fed exclusively by snow melt.

The lakes around us, many of which are actually reservoirs, dropped this year to less than 10 percent of their capacity before the irrigation district stopped syphoning their waters for agricultural use in mid-September. Some of them hold less than 5 percent water right now. This year, 70 percent of Oregon was in severe drought by mid-August, and some southern parts were extreme drought.

My nearly forty-year-old body feels the drought, and not only because its cells have aged in their ability to process toxins and minerals, wash them out, and replenish quickly with moisture. I don't bemoan the dry air for the cosmetic annoyance of winter dry skin alone. Mountain lakes are where families around here play. But choking wildfire smoke for months on end robbed us of the usual summer delights: weekend swimming, canoeing, and fishing.

Weeks back, we thought we would grab the Labor Day holiday, rent some watercraft, and trek up higher into the Cascades. Knowing our favorite lake started the year only half full and dropped from there, we headed forty minutes further north and into the range. I should have checked the water levels first. From our picnic table beneath the pines, the water looked low and a shade greener than usual. But we aren't very experienced at these things, and the air was blessedly clear enough to breathe at last. We'd already paid to rent the kayaks and boards, and we get so few opportunities to play as a family. So, we dragged the inflatables down to the water's edge.

Except it didn't really have an edge. Green-tinged muck sucked at our bare feet. It was gross. I thought for sure once we got a few feet from the shore, the water would clear, the snow-melt begin to refresh us and heal. The water never lost its green tinge, though. Twenty feet out, I suspected. Thirty feet out, I was sure. Our paddles were slicing through an algae bloom, a moderately toxic infection that had turned the lake into a bowl of thin pea soup. No one else was out on the lake on anything that would bring that water in contact with their skin. It was dead.

I told the kids to keep their mouths closed tight even from the paddles' splash. There would certainly be no swimming. I caved to their whining for rest, snacks, and a drink much sooner than I normally would, gave up and got us to shore, gamely offering to sink my own ankles and shins into the putrid slime in order to pull the kayaks across the thirty-foot gap from the stinking shallows past the grounded and empty dock.

I've never wanted so badly to have a bath. Clean water was, in that moment, worth more than gold.

It's not that I'm too delicate for pond muck. We swam in ponds as kids much more often than in chlorine-clear pools. My childhood church had three ponds, two in its backyard filled with blue-gill, small-mouth bass, and carp, which we used for camp canoe races, muck fights, and baptisms, too. That congregation practiced immersion, usually on Easter, which even at its latest in north-central Ohio meant the water was icy cold. I watched many of these, shivering in my coat knowing I was still much warmer than the youth or adult getting dunked three times under that water we raced canoes across during summer camp.

Part of the idea was to enact a cleansing despite the ways pond scum and weeds clung to the old clothes picked by the soaked initiates.

One of my favorite church nerd things to tell unsuspecting people—whether preparing for baptism or just learning about Lent—is that baptismal candidates in the early church would not bathe or change their clothes for the weeks of penitence, fasting, learning, and prayer leading up to Easter. "Then," I say, relishing the drama, "at the Easter Vigil, they would take off those old, smelly clothes, go down into the water for baptism, and then come back up out of the water to be wrapped in a new, fresh robe." It's the spiritual antecedent, I guess, for those Saturday night baths of lore and my rural youth. It's also the nearly unrecognizable origin of our contemporary customs of white baptismal outfits and a new Easter dress.

Across the centuries of making meaning from this multivalent sacrament, washing away the bad is only one stream. There are also those waters of primordial creation, the waters divided to make a way out of slavery and, of course those womb waters of birth. Water that seals a blessing that names us Beloved. Before we've done a single thing, we are bathed in the waters of love.

Both sides of my family were infant sprinklers, as the congregations I've served have been, too. I'll spare you the lengthy theological rationales. I do still love imagining what it feels like to go all the way in, to let the water slosh above you and seal you in to the magical, noise-softened world beneath the surface, even for a few moments. On the rare occasion I get to play in a pool now, I try it, curling up in a ball with my goggled eyes skyward to watch the surface drift farther away, water wrapping every inch of me, holding me, buoying me.

When I get the chance to bless and welcome a body into the family of Jesus these days, I invite children and elders alike to crowd close around the font, and then I pour the water so liberally and enthusiastically it splashes onlookers, too. Depending on their age, the shock comes mostly as delight. People actually get wet. The littlest ones shriek and jump back, extending their arms in front of themselves to receive the gift, mouths open and eyes alive like on those hot days jumping through waterfalls made by a water hose in the yard.

Near the end of *People of the Book*, Geraldine Brooks's fictional story about the Sarajevo Haggadah, a young Jewish girl wades into a body of water with her infant nephew in her arms. Her brother had converted to Christianity to marry, and yet it didn't save him from torture and murder by the Spanish Inquisition.

The young woman holds the infant in the water for a moment, then pushes him under and lets go.

I thought at first she had drowned him.

In the next beat it becomes clear this isn't a death, though. It is a rebirth.

Her release is only momentary. Using the sea as a convert's mikvah, the requisite living water, she reclaims the baby boy's Jewish heritage and faith. He is reborn through the water, reconnected to the story of the people liberated and led out of slavery through the Red Sea.

Perhaps this is why in the Eastern church the big epiphany is not about wise ones wandering to find an infant monarch beneath a celestial anomaly, but that moment both ordinary and extraordinary when Jesus rises out of the river water like everyone else to be marked with essential blessing, to hear those words, "You are my child, the Beloved. In you I find happiness."[2]

Our bodies need water. Spiritually and physically, water changes us, heals us, nourishes us, restores our beauty, gives us life. We thirst for refreshment, yes. Parched throats cannot sing praise. But the skin thirsts, too, for purification.

---

2. Mark 1:11 (CEB, adapted).

Baptism

what civil religion can capture the feeling of kneeling
in a funeral chapel dusty from months of disuse
kneeling eight or ten feet back
from the cardboard box
to keep the pandemically required distance and also
to respect the six-foot-tall nineteen-year-old
whose body rested finally on the gurney
his fileted insides duly investigated
by the coroner now contained
in a zippered orange bag

the white mortuary manager insisted too many times
his mother did not want to see him that way and still
remained wrong a mother herself
even Mary needed to caress the flesh
she had carried inside knitted together
herself with aromatic oil and tenderness

so the women went with her carrying spices and ointments
removed the lid unzipped the bag
sang to the Father and the Son in French while
anointing him head to foot that
the last words spoken over his blood and bone
before they burned might be love
and not
"Turn that damn music down!"

Purification

ahara. It means "purification" in Hebrew. It's the name for the ritual that purifies the body with water following death. In traditional Jewish communities, the specially trained *chevra kadisha* perform this ritual, first asking the deceased's forgiveness for any indignity they might commit in preparing the body for burial. With warm water and washcloths, they wash the body, immerse it three times in water, and wrap it in a simple shroud.

Islam requires burial as soon as possible after death. Muslims also use water ritually to cleanse the body, washing it three times at least. Close family members of the same sex—or the deceased's spouse—can perform the washing, called *ghusl,* moving from upper right to upper left sides of the body and from there to the lower right and lower left sides. If after three washings the body is not clean, the pattern can be repeated an odd number of times. Three hair braids for women. Three large white sheets under the body to be wrapped into a shroud.

Where modern funeral homes still wheel caskets into Christian sanctuaries for their final blessing, a white baptismal pall draped over the casket serves as a remnant and reminder of those three dunks in the water that gave the departed their most essential identity in "the name of the Father, and the Son, and of the Holy Spirit."

Is it an accident these three related faiths purify their members through water in such related ways?

Water on skin. One human washing another. A sacred task.

"Would you wash me?" I ask Adam late one night in the dark.

Whether it was a particularly heavy experience supporting a traumatically bereaved family that day or the near brush with mortality enveloping our community like a thick valley fog mid-pandemic, I'm still not sure what inspired my morbid pillow talk.

"Would you wash me when I've died?" I asked. "You can think about it. You don't have to answer now. I just . . . I don't want a stranger's hands on me. I want those final touches to be from loving hands."

Only a few families in my ministry to date have planned and chosen to wash their loved one's body in this final act of care. Like good American consumers, we've largely outsourced that work just like we now rent the "parlors" and "homes" in which we receive the visitation and condolences of friends. But not a single family I've known to give that final intimate purification has regretted it.

It's one of Brenda's favorite memories of her grandson Cruz, who lived for only nine days after his birth.

"Removing the gluey paste from his hair and washing his body gave us normalcy and intimacy," she writes me. "We could finally let him feel our love through our touch, and it was finally something we could do to care for him and not have to rely on the professionals providing so much else of his care. I think this was especially important for Cruz's dad, who was probably a bit more intimidated by the hospital setting. He had a lot of fun playing with hair styles on our very hairy boy. Although we only had nine days with him, by bathing him and dressing him we saw his body change too (he gained one pound due to his mom's powerful breast milk!) So again, that simple act gave us insight into what was happening with him."

Perhaps this feels easier to do with infants, who are already so dependent and reliant on adult hands to hold them. Brenda's daughter, who is a nurse, likes working the night shift because that's when these quieter and more intimate acts of care can be performed.

Washing another person forms a bond of tenderness, acceptance, and care. The first thing a hospice nurse said to a friend moving into a hospice center was, "Let's wash your hair."

"So many think of it as 'undignified' to have someone else bathe you," Brenda writes, "but when you are sick and especially when possibly dying, having the opportunity to feel clean and refreshed and with loving hands is a beautiful thing."[1]

That's why I asked Adam late that long night after I had seen my fill of pain and grief and death.

He said yes.

Then we held each other as long as we could.

---

1. Personal correspondence with author.

Glad Streams

One day I put my hands in the mighty Colorado River, the river that helped carve the greatest gash in the earth humans have ever seen, a wound from which the Navajo believe all of life emerged.

I submerged my hands and my feet, so cold they burned before turning numb. I put my hands and feet in the Colorado's clear shallows pebbled with red rocks and lined with greenery on a desert heat warning day to mark a new season, a starting over, a rebirth.

I'd wanted to mark a new beginning in a mikvah that one of our local rabbis offered to a couple of us interfaith colleagues coming out on the other side of serious spiritual trials. I was going to ask to do it on Good Friday. Or Holy Saturday. Poetic, right?

After four or six—or maybe forty—years listening to the story my body was trying to tell me, I was ready to put the trauma behind, submerge my body, and wipe my hands clean. All done. Not that I'm ungrateful, God, but can we wrap this lesson up?

A month before my tentatively scheduled rebirth, our governor issued a "stay home" order in the wake of a novel coronavirus sickening hundreds of thousands and killing many around the globe.

No more steam room. No more communal pools. No more touching people we didn't live with or getting closer than six feet. The only baptism I'd get that Holy Week were the tears that fell after signing off from Palm Sunday worship, livestreamed from my office, the stress of tech glitches making my hands shake so much they kept stopping and starting music videos.

Weeks stretched into months, and rather than healing, holy pools, I could only give my body the anti-anxiety medicine a doctor had prescribed more than a year ago but that I hadn't been ready then to take.

By June, we were desperate for a family holiday and decided to keep our camping reservation at the Grand Canyon, toting our own shower tent and paint-bucket toilet to minimize the risks of getting or giving that microscopic virus. Completely unplugged from the internet, we sat in the shade of pinyon pines, watched baby elk squawk for their mothers, and tried to stay smarter than the campsite scavenging ravens in a nearly deserted campground.

All around, the Navajo and Hopi nations suffered from the virus.

I noticed historical placards telling somewhat sanitized stories of our federal government displacing the Havasupai from the popular hiking oasis now called Indian Garden when they realized that the most valuable treasure in the canyon was not the uranium for which white people had started to mine, but the water that uranium mining endangered. I prayed for repentance and reparation, asking, "How can we make amends?"

We would have to stop stealing the water first.

Weeks earlier, the president of Navajo Nation and council members of the Havasupai urged the National Park Service to keep Grand Canyon parks closed during the pandemic since they bring so many tourists through the bordering native communities. The nations were seeing thousands of infections.

"We appreciate the economic benefits that tourists bring," President Jonathan Nez told a US legislative committee. "However, we continue to fear the potential negative impacts of reopening the state governments and parks."[1] Clicking through websites, we weighed whether we could keep our tenting reservation without causing more harm. Would it help to put some of our vacation budget in Navajo hands? Or would our family of four's impact bring that much more strain? Honor the closures, keep to ourselves, stay respectful. If they were open, perhaps we could buy takeout at the trading post, suffering in the lockdowns as much or more than every other small business dependent on tourism. At Navajo Bridge we passed roadside stands and the market empty of vendors. We bought our annual family Christmas ornament from the lone Navajo craftsman sitting in the sweltering sun.

---

1. Staff reports and Associate Press, "Navajo President Urges National Park Service to Keep Grand Canyon Closed," *Navajo-Hopi Observer*, June 3, 2020.

When we finally made it to the place we could dip our toes in the canyon-carving river, two local Navajo were packing up red and blue camp chairs and plastic coolers, the morning's fishing gear.

"How's the fishing?" I asked.

"We didn't catch any today," they said. "Maybe tomorrow will be better."

Not fifty feet away, two companies with leases to lead white water rafting trips down the Colorado piled white vacationers into large rafts. Signs declared private watercraft prohibited on that stretch of river. I couldn't have put my kayak in. But those companies could. In the midst of a pandemic.

This was not how I wanted to finish my book. I dreamed an ending in the living water of my friend's mikvah, not wrestling with white supremacy's commercialized consumption of healing streams. I wanted to put the embodied trauma behind, move on, begin a new chapter. Yet the viral pandemic wreaking havoc brought more: my shaking hands, a rehooked nervous system, anxiety attacks in restaurants and bathrooms. The virus infected even those of us who had not fallen sick.

And yet. That complicated Colorado River is where I put my hands and feet. Toes treading carefully over those ancient stones for fear of fishhooks. It wasn't the baptism I wanted. It would have to do.

A wound, one of my teachers said years ago, can become a womb.

"There is a river whose streams make glad the city of God, a holy habitation of the most high."[2]

Holy Habitation: this river and the body washed in it.

---

2. Psalm 46:4.

Epilogue: Confession

n the chapel of a convent along the lower Wisconsin bank of the Mississippi, a group of sisters keeps the longest continuous adoration of the blessed sacrament in North America. Twenty-four hours a day, seven days a week, 365 days of the year, at least two nuns are offering prayers and blessings before wafer and wine that, through the eyes of faith, have become Jesus's flesh and blood, his body.

They are there right now, in fact, in the Maria Angelorum Chapel of St. Rose Convent—at least two Franciscan Sisters of Perpetual Adoration. As long as a tornado hasn't struck in the time between my writing and your reading, or another fire like the one a statue of Michael the Archangel miraculously stopped in 1923. For 140 years these women have been lifting up the prayers and pleas of humans across the planet. They get thirty thousand requests a year.

"It's the body of Christ praying for the body of Christ in the presence of the body of Christ," one sister says.[1]

This is not my tradition. As a Protestant, I was steeped in an anti-Catholicism that scoffed at such practices as superstitious, magical, and idolatrous. But as you've already heard, Augustine and I no longer get along. I renounced that theological inheritance, though it takes daily practice to keep working it out of my body and blood.

Lately I've been thinking Jesus is lucky to have perpetual attention given to his body—not the multimedia assault on its frailties and imperfections all our flesh and bones increasingly endure, but prayers of loving adoration. What if every body on this planet had that kind of attention? Two sisters, offering only and always blessing, around the clock?

---

1. Dan Stockman, "140 Years of Perpetual Adoration Are Unbroken by Fire, Flood or War," Global Sisters Report, July 23, 2018, *www.globalsistersreport.org*.

When I first began to startle at divinity shining through human skin and discolored nails, I believed death was the doorway. My friend Rosalind says this makes sense.

"Rarely do we get to contemplate a body. It's awkward for everyone, unless one of the people in the room is dead and doesn't care."

I was slightly mistaken, however. Not at death alone does the holy enter into our material existence. This body is the door. These bones, this flesh, this blood. Without a body what is death but an abstraction, an idea? Without blood that pools, without heart muscles that stop or neurons that flash—warm ischemic time. In this body, we pass into the holy, cross from profane to sacred and back across the threshold again. For that reason, I will adore the body.

Mine and yours.

Dirt and stone and bone falling through our fingers.

With our bodies, we thee worship.